MOTOR LEARNING:

An Experiential Guide for Teachers

E. Doris McKinney

University of North Carolina
at Greensboro
Greensboro, North Carolina

Mouvement Publications, Inc.
109 E. State St.
Ithaca, N.Y. 14850

Woodstock
19 Oaks Way, Gayton
Heswall, Wirral
L60 3SP England

Woorkarrim
Lot #7 Strathmore Drive
Torquay 3228
Australia

Motor Learning: An Experiential Guide for Teachers

Copyright © 1985 by McKinney, Doris E..

Production by Sandy Sharpe

Typeset by Strehle's Computerized Typesetting, Ithaca, New York

Printed in the United States of America.

First Edition

ISBN 0-932392-25-3

Acknowledgements

Recognition and appreciation are extended to Janet M. Oussaty who composed and produced the action figures included in the Guide, to Margaret Hemingway for her patient and expert typing of the text, to Randa D. Russell for her constant encouragement, and to the many graduate and undergraduate students with whom I have had the privilege of working over many years.

Table of Contents

Preface

The notion for an Experiential Guide for Teachers of Motor Learning grew out of a perceived need for materials, ideas, and activities which teachers of undergraduate students of motor learning might find helpful to try in the classroom and/or gymnasium rather than having to use a laboratory equipped for advanced study and research. The Guide is intended as a ready reference to topics in motor learning which are important for teachers to understand and apply as they assist students in the learning and performance of motor skills.

Emphasis has been placed on active participation by the student in the learning process. Each section of the Guide has been organized to include a brief informational overview to a topic, a list of relevant terms to define or describe, questions to be answered and discussed, physical activities which exemplify and lead to practical application of the topic, and specific references to sources to be read in conjunction with the Guide, or as additions to the information included in the brief overview of each section.

The overview and orientation content of the Guide is made up of a synthesis and an adaptation of information to be found in the literature of motor learning, experimental psychology, educational psychology, and motivational psychology. Study questions and activities have been adapted or devised largely by the author from those experiences which have proven useful in teaching motor learning to undergraduates in a classroom. Sources of ideas are recognized in the reference and bibliographical lists at the end of each section.

It is hoped that, through the use of the Guide, teachers and students will understand the literature of motor learning and will be assisted in translating theoretical information into practical applications.

E. Doris McKinney
School of Health, Physical
  Education and Recreation
University of North Carolina
  at Greensboro

I. Introduction

A BRIEF HISTORY

The historical foundations of motor learning are to be found in experimental and learning psychology. During the early years, 19th century, psychologists studied motor learning as a medium through which they could observe behavior related to perception, stimulus discrimination, learning progress, practice conditions, and retention. The focus was not on the motor behavior for itself.

During the 1920's and 1930's, physical educators began to apply psychological topics, theories, and procedures to observe motor behavior involved in motor abilities and skills. The literature of the period reflects a focus on the development of tests to assess physical abilities, aptitudes, and capacities. In addition, attention was given to the application of theories of learning, developed in psychology, to the acquisition of motor skills.

A significant impetus was given to the study of motor ability and skill during World War II in the 1940's. Psychologists within the military forces directed their attention to the identification of abilities and skills needed to pilot airplanes successfully. As a result of their work, motor skill and ability topics became widespread in both the psychological and physical education literature.

Compilations of research pertinent to motor skills began to appear in the 1960's. Those compilations became the textbooks for academic courses in motor learning which were introduced in graduate schools of physical education during that period. The focus was on understanding and applying information which had been generated through the early research of psychologists and physical educators. The information pertained to problems of learning and of teaching motor skills. Attention centered on the product(s) of learning.

By the 1970's, physical educators had begun to develop theories and models of motor skill learning and performance based on cybernetics and information processing. Emphasis was placed on the process as well as on the product of motor skill acquisition and performance. While that emphasis continues to hold a central place in the study of motor learning, an additional focus is emerging. That focus is on motor control in which biomechanics, kinesiology, neurophysiology, and neuropsychology are included.

SOURCES OF INFORMATION

The many sources other than textbooks from which information for motor learning and control may be drawn are exemplified in the representative list of professional journals below. Authors whose works appear in the journals identified represent physical educators, educational, experimental, and social psychologists along with neuropsychologists, kinesiologists, exercise physiologists, neuropsysiologists, bioengineers, and biomechanists.

American Journal of Mental Deficiencies
American Journal of Physical Medicine
American Journal of Psychology
American Psychologist

Journal of Physical Education, Recreation, Dance
Journal of Human Movement Studies
Journal of Human Stress

Archives of Psychology
Attention and Performance
British Journal of Psychology
British Medical Journal
Canadian Journal of Applied Sport Sciences
Canadian Journal of Psychology
Cerebral Palsy Review
Developmental Medicine and Child Neurology
Environment and Behavior
Ergonomics
Exceptional Children
Experimental Analysis of Behavior
Experimental Neurology
Growth
Health Education
Human Factors
International Journal of Sport Psychology
Journal of Abnormal Social Psychology
Journal of American Medical Association
Journal of Applied Behavior Analysis
Journal of Applied Physiology
Journal of Applied Psychology
Journal of Child Psychology and Psychiatry
Journal of Comparative and Physiological
   Psychology
Journal of Consulting and Clinical Psychology
Journal of Educational Psychology
Journal of Experimental Psychology
Journal of Experimental Child Psychology
Journal of General Psychology

Journal of Motor Behaivor
Journal of Neuropsychology
Journal of Occupational Psychology
Journal of Personality
Journal of Sport Behavior
Journal of Sport Psychology
Journal of Sport Medicine and Physical Fitness
Journal of Supplement Abstract Service
Learning Processes
Medicine and Science in Sports
Organizational Behavior and Human
   Performance
Perceptual and Motor Skills
Physical Educator
Physical Therapy Review
Physician and Sports Medicine
Psychological Bulletin
Psychological Monographs
Psychological Review
Psychonomic Science
Psychonomic Society
Psychometrika
Psychophysiology
Quarterly Journal of Experimental Psychology
Quest
Research Quarterly for Exercise and Sport
   (formerly Research Quarterly)
School and Society
Science
Scientific American

II. Guide to Understanding Theories and Models of Physical Skill Learning

Overview and Orientation

Knowledge of learning theories and models can aid teachers in the selection of effective approaches to instruction. They provide bases for explaining, interpreting, and predicting learning behavior. While there is a difference in definitions applied to theory and to model, for practical purposes they may be used interchangeably.

Some theories have been criticized because they are either too vague or too difficult to translate into practice; others have been found to offer acceptable but limited explanations of conditions appropriate for learning, and of processes through which a learner goes.

Theories applied to skill acquisition range from those with a behavioristic emphasis on stimulus-response, as is found in classical conditioning, associationism, and operant conditioning, to those with a perceptual and cognitive focus based in gestalt psychology, to the current process descriptions offered by cybernetic and information processing explanations and models.

Among the stimulus-response theories having wide usage in skill acquisition are found those proposed by E. L. Thorndike and B. F. Skinner. Such explanations of learning place emphasis on conditions which will strengthen the association between a stimulus and a response to be learned. They are environment and product centered. Drills and repetition, reinforcement, and part to whole approaches to instruction are based on such theories.

Cognitive-perceptual explanations of learning focus on the individual. Those theories emphasize the importance of the individual's interaction with the environment. They point up the central role that perception plays in learning. Cognitive-perceptual theorists maintain that learning results from the individual's perception of relationships in a problem situation and the restructuring of those relationships to solve the problem. Practices of problem solving, concept formation, and the learning of general principles stem from cognitive theory.

With the advent of the computer, interest grew in the theories and models which held the potential for shedding light on the processes of learning rather than the environment and products. Cybernetic and information processing explanations became the center of attention. Prototypical cybernetic descriptions and models were generated using the computer terms of input, central processing, output, and feedback to refer to the human counterparts of sensory modality, brain, muscular response, and proprioceptor feedback. Figure 1 is a general, simplified example of a cybernetic model:

Cybernetic theory, with its emphasis on feedback on closed-loop control by way of the servo-mechanisms (proprioceptors) of the body, stimulated research into how movement is controlled. It helped, also, to focus attention on the operation and effect of intrinsic and extrinsic feedback (see Section VIII of the Guide). The theories of J. A. Adams (1971), N. Bernstein (1967), and K. U. Smith (1967), often cited in motor learning literature, were based on cybernetic explanations of behavior.

Currently, there exist numerous models and explanations which stem from information processing theory. The reception, transformation, and storage of information by the individual together with decision making functions are of central concern. Research is proceeding rapidly on the roles of the sensory modalities, perception, selective attention, memory, speed of processing, decision making, formu-

3

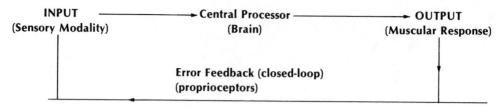

Figure 1. Simplified basic cybernetic model and equivalent human components.

lation of motor plans, control of motor responses, and feedback in the acquisition of a skill. A simplified example of an information processing model is given in Figure 2.

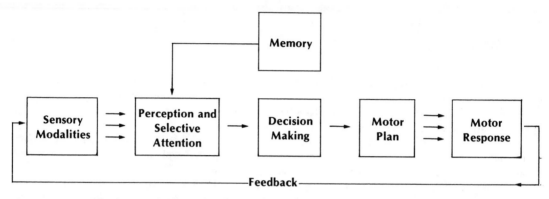

Figure 2. Simplified basic model of information processing.

Results of the research, although tentative, are offering teachers new ideas about the process of learning. They identify, in a graphic way, points in the process where learners may differ or may encounter difficulties. Some evidence accumulated to date can be translated into effective instructional procedures to facilitate perception, selective attention, memory storage and retrieval, decision making, and the formulation of motor plans.

A detailed presentation and discussion of the numerous models of information processing developed is beyond the scope of this Guide. Explanations offered by Gentile (1972), Marteniuk (1976), Schmidt (1982), Welford (1976), and Whiting (1969) would be of interest to teachers of physical skills. Their works are cited in the bibliography.

An overview and orientation to theory would not be complete without calling attention to the stage theory by Fitts (1964). According to the theory, a learner moves through three stages, namely cognitive, associative, and autonomous, as proficiency in a skill is developed. Fitts not only described characteristics of the learner during each stage, but also provided guides to instruction to facilitate passage of the learner through each stage. A full discussion of the theory may be found in Fitts (1964) and Magill (1980).

Recent developments in theory and models are emphasizing the neurophysiological and neuropsychological mechanisms involved in the production and control of movement. The focus is on proprioception, muscular response, and cortical functions. Implications for instructions, based on the theories and modes of control, are beginning to emerge.

KEY WORDS TO DEFINE OR DESCRIBE

Association (Fixation Stage)	Cognitive Learning	Cybernetics
Associationism	Cognitive-Perceptual Theory	Decision Making
Autonomous Stage	Cognitive Stage	Feedback
Central Processing	Cognitive Theory	Gestaltism
Classical Conditioning	Connectionism	Information Processing
Closed-loop Control	Cortical	Input

Instrumental Learning
Learning
Learning Theory
Memory
Model
Motor Plan
Neurophysiological
Neuropsychological

Operant Conditioning
Output
Perception
Process
Processing Speed
Product
Proprioceptors
Selective Attention

Sensory Modalities
Servomechanisms
Shaping
Single Channel
Stimulus Response (S-R)
Theory

QUESTIONS FOR DISCUSSION

1. Interpret the following symbols: S-R; s-O-r; $S \begin{smallmatrix} R \\ \rightleftarrows \\ R \end{smallmatrix}$; $S \left\{ \begin{smallmatrix} s\text{-}r \\ s\text{-}r \\ s\text{-}r \\ s\text{-}r \\ s\text{-}r \\ s\text{-}r \end{smallmatrix} \right\} R$

2. Cite briefly the contributions of the following theorists to the understanding and explanation of learning: Pavlov, Guthrie, Thorndike, Hull, Gagne, and Skinner.

3. Different teachers emphasize different methods and techniques in the teaching of skills. Review the following examples of teaching procedures and techniques, then identify the major theory(ies) by which the teacher appears to be guided:

   a. The teacher who emphasizes "drill(s)" to develop a preferred way of performing.

   b. The teacher who seeks transfer by pointing up similarities among types of activities.

   c. The teacher who teaches for transfer through knowledge of principles and concepts.

   d. The teacher who is concerned primarily with providing students with information on their performance errors while action is in process.

   e. The teacher who practices an isolated skill, then includes that skill within the context of a larger whole and eventually within the total game, dance, or gymnastic event context.

4. What conditions and processes of learning do the above types of theories appear to interpret well for physical skill learning? What conditions and processes do not appear to be accounted for by the theories?

5. Cite briefly the contributions of the following theorists: Koffka, Wertheimer, Tolman, Snygg and Combs.

6. What conditions and processes of learning do the above types of theories appear to interpret well for physical skill learning? What conditions and processes do not appear to be accounted for by the theories?

7. Some cybernetic and information processing models are static, some dynamic. Some are linear in design, others are circular, and still others are irregular in pattern. Linear models usually take forms such as those in Figure 3.

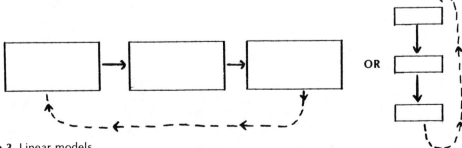

Figure 3. Linear models.

Circular models usually appear as either a partial or complete circle of component parts. See Figure 4.

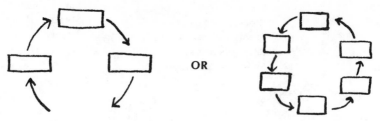

Figure 4. Circular models.

Irregular patterns may take a variety of forms. The form depends on the image that the creator of the pattern wishes to establish. Some may be modeled after the total human body or selected segments of the body, such as in Figure 5.

Figure 5. Irregular models.

Find and diagram at least two models of each type. Label all component parts.

8. What conditions and processes of learning do the models appear to explain well for physical skill learning? What conditions and processes are not explained well?

9. What adjustments can be recommended to modify the models?

10. What is the meaning of "neurophysiological basis of learning"?

11. What contribution does neurophysiological functioning make to our understanding of the process of learning?

12. What structures of the body are of major concern in the neurophysiological explanation of the process of learning and performing?

13. Are there apparent relationships between the "neurophysiological basis" and cybernetic theory? Explain.

14. Explain, by applying neurophysiological, cybernetic and information processing understandings, why cues and instructions to performers such as:

> "Get a longer back swing" — Tennis
> "Get half-flexion of ankle and knee, then extend *quickly*" — Jumping
> "Tuck your head *tightly* to the chest and make a ball of your body" — Forward roll

may help the performer/learner to execute the movement effectively.

15. Often a change in a piece of equipment, such as changing from one type of tennis racquet to another, may result in more effective performance. Apply neurophysiological and cybernetic information to explain why improvement may occur.

16. Most information processing models include multiple vectors (arrows) to illustrate the number of stimuli involved in "Input"; however, only a single vector leads into "Processing." What does the single vector represent? What implication does that representation have for the giving of instructions?

ACTIVITIES

1. Role play the teaching of a skill of your choice (ex. catching a ball, throwing a ball, a basketball shot, a hockey pass, a lacrosse cradle, etc.) to at least one other person. Determine the theory(ies) upon which your procedure of presentation appears to be based. Evaluate this procedure in the light of S-R, cognitive, neurophysiological, cybernetic, and information processing explanations.

2. Demonstrate (do not verbalize) to a learner an overhand softball throw to a target 40 feet away. Both speed and accuracy are important. In addition to body and foot position be sure to include in your demonstration: the correct position of elbow on windup, the position of the ball in the hand, a release with a wrist snap and fingers following through to point to the target. Immediately following the demonstration, ask the beginner to state the details observed. How many details were seen? Were the details observed critical components of the throw? Account for the beginner's response according to information processing explanations.

3. Observe a batter at home plate as a pitcher releases a ball to him/her. List the decisions that the batter must make in attempting to hit the ball. According to information processing models, what components are involved in those decisions?

4. Select a volunteer learner from a group. Send the volunteer out of the room while you explain to the group what the learner will be expected to achieve thorough "shaping of successive approximations." The learner is expected to place the ball between the feet, hold it tightly with the ankles, and convert it from a ground ball to an aerial ball by jumping up, releasing the ball from between the ankles and catching it. Demonstrate the action to the group. See Figure 6.

Figure 6. Conversion of ground ball to aerial ball.

Have the volunteer learner return, then explain to learner and to group the task as follows: "We have selected a skill for you to perform with this soccer ball. You will have to determine what it is by trying out different movements. Each time your movements are those involved in the skill as it should be performed, we will say "correct," if the movements are not correct, we won't say anything." Instruct the learner to begin. Observe the response. Did the learner achieve the skill? What purpose did the no response serve? Identify and discuss the theory of learning applied.[1]

5. Work with a partner, seated at a desk, with one of the pair blindfolded. The "seeing" partner places a small object (pencil, eraser, block, etc.) just in front of the blindfolded individual on the table. Instruct the individual who cannot see to pick up the object immediately as the blindfold is removed. Remove the blindfold. Observe the action. What part of the action is voluntary control? What part is under involuntary or subcortical control? Apply a cybernetic or neurophysiological explanation for the action. Try to develop a schematic "model" or diagram of the structures of the body involved. Label it.

6. With eyes open, elbow straight, arm hanging by the side of the body, flex the elbow to approximately 20 degrees. With eyes closed, try to replicate the movement to the 20 degree angle. Explain the success or lack of success. What theory(ies) may offer support for your explanation?

7. Try the positioning in (6) above using approximately 10 or 30 degrees of flexion with eyes closed and with a partner placing the arm at the selected angle. The partner should then take the arm back to the starting position. With eyes still closed, try to replicate the 10 or 30 degree angle. Explain your success or lack of success. What theory(ies) may offer support for your explanation?

8. Work with a partner. One of the pair with eyes closed so as not to see the object to be used. Flex the elbow to a 90 degree angle with the palm of the hand supinated (facing palm up). On the signal "Now," partner is instructed to open his/her eyes. The partner with the object (indoor shot or similar weight) immediately drops the weight or places it quickly into the upturned palm. See Figure 7. Observe what happens. Explain your observation.

Figure 7. Partners with heavyweight.

9. Try (8) above with eyes open and with knowledge of the approximate weight of the object. Explain what happens and why? How does the action differ from that observed in (8) above?

10. Study an information processing model, then analyze a skill (refer to Section VII of the Guide) and teach it according to the model. What parts of the model are under your control?

11. Use 5x8 cards. Print on each card one component of an information processing model, such as in Figure 8. Give one card to each student. Instruct students to form the model by standing in the correct position as related to all other components. Once the "human" model has been formed, provide the sensory input with a stimulus, such as a ball thrown at a 45° angle into the air to be caught by the "motor output." Each component of the "human" model then role plays in quick succession the function of that component.

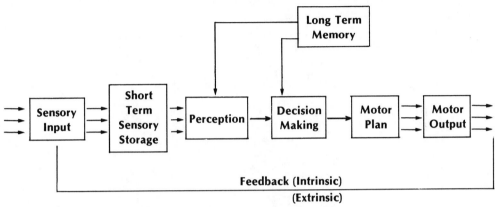

Figure 8. Suggested information processing model.

12. Observe a beginner and an advanced performer in the execution of skills in a game such as basketball. Describe the differences observed. Compare your description to that given by Fitts in his stage theory. What behaviors of learners are important indicators of their stage(s) of proficiency?

CREDITS

[1]From D. Watson (1981). Shaping by successive approximation. In L.T. Benjamin & K.D. Lowman (Eds.). *Activities handbook for the teaching of psychology* (p. 60). Washington, DC: American Psychological Association. Copyright 1981 by the American Psychological Association. Adapted by permission of the publisher.

BIBLIOGRAPHY

Adams, J. A. (1971). A closed-loop theory of motor learning. *Journal of Motor Behavior, 3,* 11-149.

Annet, J. (1969). *Feedback.* Baltimore: Penquin Books.

Bernstein, N. (1967). *The coordination and regulation of movements.* New York: Pergamon Press.

Bigge, M. L. (1971). *Learning theories for teachers.* New York: Harper and Row.

Dickinson, J. D. (1974). *Proprioceptive control of human movement.* London: Lepus Books.

Fitts, P. M. (1964). Perceptual-Motor Learning. In A. W. Melton (Ed.), *Categories of human learning.* New York: Academic Press.

Gagne, R. (1970). *The conditions of learning.* New York: Holt, Rinehart, and Winston.

Gardner, E. B. (1969). Proprioceptive reflexes and their participation in motor skills. *Quest, XII,* 1-25.

Garry, R. & Kingsley, H. L. (1970). *The nature and conditions of learning.* Englewood Cliffs: Prentice-Hall.

Gentile, A. M. (1972). A working model of skill acquisition. *Quest, XVII,* 1-23.

Hilgard, E. R. & Bower, G. E. (1966). *Theories of learning.* New York: Appleton-Century-Crofts.

Kerr, R. (1982). *Psychomotor learning* (pp. 20-50). New York: W. B. Saunders College Publishing.

Legge, D. (1970). *Skills.* Baltimore: Penguin Books.

Magill, R. (1980). *Motor learning: Concepts and applications* (pp. 49-62). Dubuque, IA: W. C. Brown.

Pease, D. A. (1977). A teaching model for motor skill acquisition. *Motor Skills: Theory into Practice, 1,* 104-112.

Robb, A., Catelli, L., Doods, P. & Manahan, J. (1981). *Motor learning: Basic stuff series I* (pp. 1-10). Reston, VA., American Alliance of Health Physical Education, Recreation and Dance.

Robb, M. (1972). *The dynamics of motor skill acquisition.* Englewood Cliffs: Prentice-Hall.

Rushall, B. & Seidentop, D. (1972). *The development and control of behavior in sports and physical education.* Philadelphia: Lea and Febiger.

Singer, R. N. (1980). *Motor learning and human performance.* New York: MacMillan.

Singer, R. N. (1982). *The learning of motor skills* (pp. 22-23). New York: MacMillan.

Smith, K. U. (1967). Cybernetic foundations of a physical behavior science. *Quest, VIII,* 26-82.

Stallings, L. (1982). *Motor learning: From theory to practice* (pp. 23-41). St. Louis: C. V. Mosby.

Stelmach, G. (1976). *Motor control: Issues and trends.* New York: Academic Press.

Watson, D. (1981). Shaping by successive approximations. In L. T. Benjamin & K. D. Lowman (Eds.), *Activities handbook for the teaching of psychology,* Washington, DC: American Psychological Association.

Welford, A. T. (1968). *Fundamentals of skill.* London: Methueh.

Whiting, H. T. A. (1969). *Acquiring ball skill.* Philadelphia: Lea and Febiger.

III. Guide to Understanding Motor Abilities

OVERVIEW AND ORIENTATION

The focus of this section of the Guide is on abilities; however, due to the tendency of many practitioners to employ the terms "ability" and "skill" as if they were synonymous, it is important to clarify the difference between the two. Motor skill, as defined within motor learning, refers to the organization and execution of selected movement patterns in a particular temporal and spatial sequence in order to accomplish a specific purpose. For example, an overhand softball throw to a target or to a base is a skill. Analysis of what is needed to execute that throw might reveal balance, dynamic strength, wrist and finger flexibility, and speed of movement. The components identified in the analysis are abilities. Abilities underly skills. They are said to be innate and enduring, but subject to some influence of experience and learning. Skills, however, are the product of learning and practice. The identification of abilities can aid teachers to organize instructional and practice sessions to facilitate, to the extent possible, the emergence of abilities needed to acquire and perform a variety of skills.

Motor abilities have been found to be relatively specific both within the individual and within the motor task. At one time investigators sought evidence for a general motor ability. Such an attribute was defined as one which would underly many different motor tasks. To date, despite extensive research, no such general ability has been identified; instead, investigators have found many relatively specific abilities. The work of Fleishman (1972) resulted in the identification of psychomotor and gross motor abilities. From more than 200 tasks, Fleishman found psychomotor factors, such as reaction time, rate control, response orientation, speed of arm movement, wrist-finger speed, arm-hand steadiness, manual and finger dexterity, multilimb coordination, control precision, and aiming. The gross motor abilities identified included dynamic strength, static strength, explosive strength, trunk strength, extent flexibility, dynamic flexibility, gross body coordination, and stamina. Guilford (1958) found abilities which he designated as impulsion, speed, static precision, dynamic precision, coordination, and flexibility. Each of the factors was found to be made up of several subfactors which appeared to be specific to either the gross body, the trunk, the limbs, or the hands and fingers. The recent emphasis on information processing theory has led to some attempts to identify and name perceptual, decision making, and emotional abilities as well as motor ones.

While efforts to identify abilities continue, at present it appears that a general motor ability does not exist; rather, there are many specific factors. Further, specific skills seem to require specific abilities. Skills may require different sets of abilities, or they may use similar sets ordered in different ways. In addition, abilities possessed by one person may not be highly related within that person; for example, an individual who possesses trunk strength may not have a high degree of explosive strength, or one who has fast reaction time may not show fast speed of movement. Despite the specificity, some writers (Singer, 1980) state that most physical skills require the abilities involved in strength, speed, and coordination.

The interest in the identification of abilities is paralleled by a focus on their role as predictors of achievement of learners. Prediction studies, however, show that abilities which appear to be important at the beginning of learning are not the same as those emerging late in learning. Fleishman and Hempel

(1954) found that visual factors, perceptual speed, and spatial relations applied at the beginning of learning a complex coordination task gave way to a rate of movement and coordination specific to the task in late learning trials. Fleishman and Rich (1963) observed that an emphasis on vision in early learning trials was replaced by kinethesis during late trials. Explanations to account for the failure of ability tests to predict achievement include the observation that the tests assess only the abilities involved in the test rather than the factors underlying the task to be learned.

KEY WORDS TO DEFINE OR DESCRIBE

Ability
Agility
Aptitude
Balance
Coordination
Dynamic Flexibility
Endurance
Explosive Strength
Extent Flexibility
Flexibility
General Ability
General Aptitude
General Motor Ability
Kinethesis
Motor Ability

Motor Aptitude
Motor Capacity
Motor Educability
Motor Fitness
Physical Fitness
Power
Prediction
Reaction Time
Skill
Skill Tests
Speed
Speed of Movement
Static Strength
Strength

QUESTIONS FOR DISCUSSION

1. Differentiate between the meaning of the term "skill" and the term "ability."

2. Compare the abilities identified by Fleishman and Guilford. Which of the abilities appear to be common to both?

3. What types of tests and/or observations were used by Fleishman and Guilford? Evaluate them as tests of ability in accordance with the definition or description of an ability?

4. Define and differentiate among motor ability tests, motor educability tests, motor capacity tests, motor fitness tests, and motor skills tests.

5. How do the test items in each of the types of tests in (4) above differ?

6. Motor ability and skill tests are used frequently in physical education classes to classify students and evaluate their achievement. Based on conclusions of prediction research, comment on that use of tests.

7. Some writers have concluded that children demonstrate general ability more than adults do. Explain why this observation may be correct.

8. If there is no general ability, explain how it is possible for a performer to be superior in many motor skills included in different games and sports.

9. What are the instructional implications of the fact that the abilities applied at advanced levels of learning and performing are different from those employed at beginning levels?

ACTIVITIES

1. Describe or diagram as many tests as you can find which have been employed to determine motor abilities.

2. Sit-ups and push-ups are both measures of strength. Administer each to five students. Have each person perform as many sit-ups as possible; after a period of rest (10 minutes), have the same person perform as many push-ups as possible. Rank order the five students according to the number of sit-ups, then push-ups, that they have been able to do. Find the rank difference correlation (Rho). Explain the result.

Subject	Sit-up Rank	Push-up Rank	D	D^2
A	_____	_____	_____	_____
B	_____	_____	_____	_____
C	_____	_____	_____	_____
D	_____	_____	_____	_____
E	_____	_____	_____	_____
			ΣD^2	_____

$$Rho = 1 - \frac{6(\Sigma D^2)}{N(N^2-1)}$$

3. Work in partners. Use a stopwatch. One performs while the other times. Perform a stork stand by standing with weight on one foot, placing the free foot on the inside of the knee of the supporting leg. Place hands on hips. Keep eyes open. Maintain balance as long as possible. Balance is lost when the foot supporting the body moves to regain position. Watch should be started when a balance is struck, stopped when foot moves. Record the time. See Figure 9.

Figure 9. The stork stand.

Try the same stunt in (3) above with the eyes closed. Record the time.

Try the same stunt in (3) above with eyes open, but take the weight on the tiptoe of the supporting foot. Balance is lost if heel touches the floor or if toe moves. Time as above.

13

As in (2) above collect time scores on five students, rank order the results and correlate eyes open, eyes closed with whole foot on floor. Correlate eyes open with whole foot, eyes open on tiptoe. Based on your understanding of the specificity of abilities, explain the result obtained.

4. As in (2) above, using five students, direct them to perform as many sit-ups as possible in *one* minute. Rest five minutes, then perform as many squat thrusts as possible in *one* minute. See Figure 10. Rank order the results. Identify the abilities required to perform the two tasks.

Figure 10. Sit up.

5. Perform the following movement patterns in rapid succession (See Figure 11):

Cut step forward and sideward: (count each change as 1, 2, 3, 4)
1 — kick left foot forward, weight on right foot.
2 — place weight on left, kick right foot forward.
3 — place weight on right foot, kick left foot to side.
4 — place weight on left foot, kick right foot to side.

Repeat several times.

Then try: The Four Step Schottische "slide, cut, leap, hop." (Count each change as 1, 2, 3, 4 in 4/4 time. (See Instruction, Section VIII of Guide). See Figure 12.
1 — Slide left foot diagonally forward, weight on right foot.
2 — Cut away left foot by closing right to left and taking weight quickly on right foot.
3 — Leap onto the left foot.
4 — Hop on the left foot.
Repeat beginning with (1) above starting with the right foot. Identify the ability(ies) being applied in those patterns. Does proficiency in one pattern insure proficiency in the other pattern? Explain. Identify the primary ability exemplified in the exercise.

6. Refer to Fleishman's list of *gross motor abilities,* then analyze the following skills to determine the abilities involved in them: (See Task Analysis, Section VII of Guide).
    a. Start of a sprint race
    b. Weightlifting
    c. Touching the floor with hands with knees straight
    d. Basketball dribbling

14

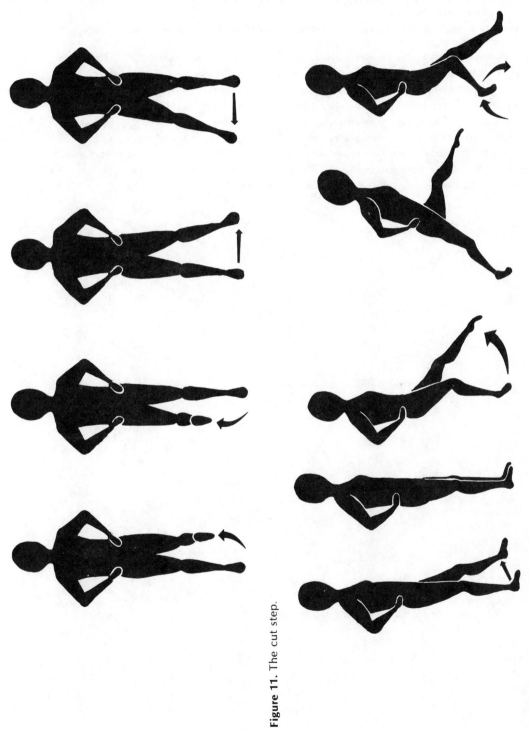

Figure 11. The cut step.

Figure 12. The four-step Schottische.

BIBLIOGRAPHY

Cratty, B. J. (1973). *Teaching of motor skills* (pp. 21-36). Englewood Cliffs: Prentice-Hall.

Cratty, B. J. (1974). *Movement behavior and motor learning.* Philadelphia: Lea and Febiger.

Fleishman, E. A. (1972). On the relationship between abilities, learning, and human performance. *American Psychologist, 27,* 1017-1031.

Fleishman, E. A. & Hempel, W. E. (1954). Changes in factor structure of a complex psychomotor test as a function of practice. *Psychometrika, 19,* 239-252.

Fleishman, E. A. & Rich, S. (1963). Role of kinesthetic and spatial visual ability in perceptual-motor learning. *Journal of Experimental Psychology, 56,* 6-11.

Garry, R. & Kingsley, H. (1970). *The nature and conditions of learning.* Englewood Cliffs: Prentice-Hall.

Guilford, J. P. (1958). A system of psychomotor abilities. *American Journal of Applied Psychology, 71,* 164-174.

Hinrichs, J. R. (1970). Ability correlates in learning a psychomotor task. *Journal of Applied Psychology, 54,* 56-64.

Kleinman, M. (1983). *The acquisition of motor skill* (pp. 173-192). Princeton, NJ: Princeton Book Company.

Jones, M. B. (1962). Practice as a process of simplification. *Psychological Review, 69,* 274-294.

Schmidt, R. A. (1981). *Motor control and learning* (pp. 396-424). Champaign, IL: Human Kinetics Publishers.

Singer, R. N. (1980). *Motor learning and human performance* (pp. 193-214; 349-354). New York: The MacMillan Company.

Singer, R. N. (1982). *The learning of motor skills* (pp. 88-93). New York: MacMillan Publishing Company.

Singer, R. N. (1972). *Readings in motor learning.* Philadelphia: Lea and Febiger.

IV. Guide to Understanding Speed of Movement and Reaction Time

OVERVIEW AND ORIENTATION

The speed or quickness with which a performer can respond is one of the characteristics associated with skillfulness in activities requiring fast execution of movement. Sprint starts and the completion of a sprint distance, or the initiation of a bat swing and its completion in batting a pitched ball are examples of movements often cited as requiring quickness.

Speed of response (the total time to respond) involves both reaction time and movement time. The time between the presentation of a signal to which to respond and the beginning of that response defines reaction time. Movement time refers to the amount of time elapsing from the beginning of a response to the completion of that response. The components of speed of response are denoted often by the equation: Reaction Time (RT) + Movement Time (MT) = Total Response Time (TRT).

Simple reaction time (SRT) involves only one signal to which to respond, while complex or choice reaction time (CRT) usually involves several signals from among which a performer must decide on the particular one to which to respond. In choice reaction time the signals may be simultaneous or follow each other in rapid succession. CRT is usually slower than SRT, therefore TRT involving the former will show less speed than the TRT which involves SRT. Often when the individual is confronted by signals occurring in rapid succession and initiates a response to one, reaction to a second one is delayed. The delay is designated as the psychological refractory period. Reaction to a signal, whether it is one requiring SRT or CRT, always consumes time. The time required is explained by the need for the stimulus (signal) to stimulate the appropriate sensory organ (visual, auditory, or cutaneous), pass over nerve tracts to the brain, and return over nerve tracts to the muscle(s) to be activated. Information processing models describe the process as receiving the stimulus, interpreting it, deciding on what to do, and, then, executing the action.

There are many instances occurring in the performance of motor skills in which SRT, CRT, and/or the psychological refractory period are involved. The pistol signal of a starter in track events exemplifies the single stimulus. The array of ball, opponents, teammates, and strategy being engaged in during a basketball game presents a situation in which several signals may exist simultaneously. A situation in which a basketball player with the ball may feint in one direction and quickly move in another exemplifies a condition in which the psychological refractory period is likely to cause a delay in effective responding by the guard opponent of the player with the ball.

Individual differences exist in reaction time. Some people are consistently faster in reacting than others. Despite the basic differences, there are several ways by which a teacher may help a learner/performer to develop effective speed and quickness. One of the important ways is to teach the performer to attend selectively only to the most important signal(s) in a given environment. Once selective attending has been developed, the environment with its numerous potentially distracting signals is simplified. The batter in baseball may selectively attend to the pitcher's release and then the ball, for example, while opposing field players, the catcher, the umpire, and the noise of the crowd are cut out of immediate consideration. Another important way to aid the development of quickness is to teach the performer to anticipate when a given signal is most likely to occur. Anticipation is made up of an estimation of the amount of time it will take to perform a movement (Effector Anticipation), the duration time of given events (Receptor Anticipation), and the regularity with which events occur (Perceptual Anticipation). An expectancy set is created which can reduce the time to receive signals, interpret them, and select an appropriate response because those processes can be initiated either slightly before or simultaneously with the occurrence of a signal. Provisions for sufficient practice in a variety of situations within a given activity should be made. Through instruction during that practice, the performer not only can learn selective attending, but also can learn to recognize signals which appear most frequently in different situations. Storage of the signals in the memory of the performer allows prediction and anticipation of what is most likely to happen next in the situations. A full discussion of this topic may be found in Kerr (1982).

In addition to teaching for selective attention and anticipation, a teacher can help a performer to improve speed by instruction in efficient and skillful ways of executing movements. The cross over step in tennis, for example, may result in faster coverage of a court from side to side than the slide step. In some instances effective movement may make up for basic individual differences in reaction time and thereby reduce the total response time of a performer whose reaction time tends to be slow.

KEY WORDS TO DEFINE OR DESCRIBE

Anticipation
Attention
Choice Reaction Time (CRT)
Components of Reaction Time
Effector
Effector Anticipation
Motor Program
Movement Time
Perception
Perceptual Anticipation

Prediction
Psychological Refractory Period
Reaction Time
Receptor
Receptor Anticipation
Selective Attention
Signal
Simple Reaction Time (SRT)
Stimulus
Total Response Time (TRT)

QUESTIONS FOR DISCUSSION

1. Why do starters of track or swimming races provide signals such as "ready-set-fire the pistol" to begin the events?

2. For the best reaction time in events described in (1) above, how much time should elapse between "Ready-set" and "firing of the pistol"? How are "false starts" related to reaction time?

3. How do personal factors (sex, age, etc.) affect reaction time?

4. How do environmental factors (intensity of signal, temperature, time of day, etc.) affect reaction time?

5. How much time on the average is required to initiate a simple response? A choice response?

6. In which component of reaction time is the greatest amount of time used?

7. Can simple reaction time be improved? If so, how?

8. Can choice reaction time be improved? If so, how?

9. Would you use simple reaction time of a performer to determine the position he/she should play on a team engaged in games requiring quickness and speed of response? Explain your answer.

10. Under what circumstances is the psychological refractory period likely to occur? Why?

11. Explain Receptor Anticipation, Effector Anticipation, Perceptual Anticipation.

12. How would you help a performer to overcome the psychological refractory period?

13. Why are practices which involve many types of situations that are likely to arise in the performance of a given skill helpful in the reduction of reaction time and total response time?

14. Select a skill, such as batting a pitched ball, and explain the application of the three Anticipation factors identified in (11) above.

ACTIVITIES

1. Form pairs of students. Each pair should have a yardstick, paper and pencil. One of the pair (the tester) places the yardstick flat, vertically against the wall, so that the 36" mark is even with a mark on the wall just above the tester's eye level. See Figure 13. The tester holds the yardstick flat against the wall with the thumb at the 34" mark. The partner of the tester (subject), standing directly in front of the yardstick, places the preferred hand flat against the wall with thumb extending over the 2" mark and focuses the eye on the 6" mark of the yardstick. The thumb should not touch the stick. The Tester says "Ready," then pauses for two seconds (count 1-1000, 2-1000 to approximate the seconds), then removes the holding thumb to let the yardstick fall. The subject attempts to stop the fall of the yardstick by pressing the thumb on the stick and against the wall as quickly as possible. Once the yardstick has been stopped, observe the point at which the thumb is pressing, noting the mark just at the upper edge of the pressing thumb. Tester records the distance that the yardstick fell. Determine the time to respond by using Table 1 and the formula:[1]:

$$\text{Time} = \sqrt{\frac{\text{(distance in inches)}}{6(32)}}$$

Was the time measured simple reaction time, choice reaction time, or total response time? Explain your answer.

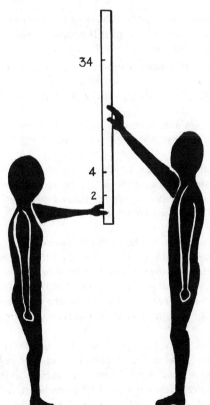

Figure 13. Lay out for reaction time test.

Table 1.
Reaction Time Conversion

Distance in Inches	Time in Seconds
1.9	.10
4.3	.15
7.7	.20
12.0	.25
17.3	.30
23.5	.35
30.7	.40

Note. From Activities handbook for the teaching of psychology (p. 203) by L. T. Benjamin and K. D. Lowman (Eds.) (1981). Washington, DC: American Psychological Association. Copyright 1981 by the American Psychological Association. Reprinted by permission of the publisher.

2. Try the activity in (1) above with the tester delaying the fall of the yardstick by 2, 4, and 7 seconds in any order. Tester can estimate number of seconds by silently counting 1-1000, 2-1000, 3-1000, etc. Compare the results of activity (2) with (1). Account for differences observed.

3. Try the activity in (1) above with partner holding both left and right hand and thumbs as described. Tester instructs partner to use left hand if the signal "SET" is given or to use right hand if signal "READY" is given. Delay the fall for only 1 second.
    a. Was the time measured simple reaction time, choice reaction time, or total response time? Explain your answer.
    b. Compare the results of activity (3) with (2) and (1) above. Account for differences observed.

4. To improve speed through anticipation, situations to be responded to should be known and recognized prior to the time an action is to be initiated.

    Work in pairs with a ball. See Figure 14. One of the pair throws the ball, the other catches it at a distance of about 15'. Instruct the catcher to turn his/her back to the thrower. Instruct the thrower to throw the ball to the catcher with any type of throw he/she wishes. As the ball is released the thrower signals with a loud "NOW." The catcher, on the signal, turns to catch the ball. Observe the response.

    Try again, but this time, the catcher faces the thrower who will throw the ball at about a 45° angle to the catcher several times. After several trials instruct the catcher to turn his/her back to the thrower. Inform the catcher that the throw just practiced will be sent with the same angle speed on the signal "NOW." Thrower sends the ball giving the signal "NOW" as the ball is released. In which of the two situations did the catcher succeed the best? Was the response to the best success faster or slower than the least successful response? Why? What type of anticipation is involved?

5. In pairs, use Section X, Activity 4, of the Guide. The catcher stands beside the thrower. The thrower will throw the ball to the target on the blackboard and the catcher will try to catch it successfully by moving to the point where it will land. Throw several balls at the target to rebound at a 45° angle to be received by the catcher. After each catch, the catcher returns to position beside the thrower. Observe the catcher's arrival time at spot to catch. Unknown by catcher, instruct the thrower to reduce the angle of the throw to about 30° or increase to 60° with the 45° angle throw inserted at any time

Figure 14. Partner catch.

(one pattern might be 30°, 60°, 45°, 45°, 60°, 60°, 30°). The catcher attempts to move to catch the ball as before. Observe the responses and compare them with the responses of the catcher when only the 45° angle was used. What cues to look for in the varied throws would you give to the catcher? Try those cues and compare all responses with respect to arrival time to catching spot and success.

6. Work in partners with a ball at a distance of about 10'. One partner of the pair *quickly* feints several times an underhand throw for which the receiving partner must reach above head height to catch. *Just as* the catcher *begins* to move the arms and hands into position to catch the high ball, the thrower will proceed *quickly* to send a fast underhand ball waist to chest-height to the catcher. Observe the response of the catcher. How successful was the catch? How quickly did the catcher adjust to the ball actually thrown? Explain.

7. In a space 40' to 50' wide, with boundary lines drawn as in Figure 15, instruct a performer beginning at one boundary line to move as fast as he can on the signal, "Ready-set-go" with left shoulder leading to the left using *slide steps*. Time the performance. (Stop watch or watch with a second hand may be used.) Have the performer return to the starting boundary line to move again. This time instruct the performer, on the signal, to lead with left shoulder and to move as fast as he/she can with a grapevine step. Time the performance. Compare the times of the slide step and grapevine step to determine which was the fastest. Account for the difference observed. How may a teacher aid a performer to develop movement speed?

8. Use a 20' clear space. Draw a line on the floor or ground. Instruct performers to take positions behind the line as if in starting blocks to begin a sprint race. Use a starter's signal "Ready-set-go." On "go" performers are to leave their line as quickly as they can. Practice the signal with the performers on line saying "Ready-set," tell the performers you will pause for two seconds (count silently "1-1000, 2-1000") before saying "go." On "go" they are to move as if beginning a race. Observe the responses. Then, try the start again. This time, without telling the runners, pause four seconds between "Ready-set" and "go" (count 1-1000, 2-1000, 3-1000, 4-1000). Observe and compare the response of the four-second pause with the two-second pause. Explain the result.

CREDITS

[1]From *Activities handbook for the teaching of psychology* (p. 203), by L.T. Benjamin and K.D. Lowman (Eds.) (1981). Washington, DC: American Psychological Association. Copyright 1981 by the American Psychological Association. Adapted by permission of the publisher.

BIBILOGRAPHY

Benjamin, L. T. & Lowman, K. D. (Eds.). (1981). *Activities Handbook for the teaching of psychology*. Washington, DC: American Psychological Association.

Cratty, B. J. (1973). *The teaching of motor skills* (p. 32). Englewood Cliffs: Prentice-Hall.

Drowatzky, J. N. (1981). *Motor Learning: Principles and practices* (pp. 128-139). Minneapolis: Burgess Publishing Company.

Keele, K. W. (1982). Component analysis and conceptions of a skill. In J. A. Scott Kelso (Ed.); *Human motor behavior: An introduction*. Hillsdale, NJ: Lawrence Erlbaum Associates.

Kerr, R. (1982). *Psychomotor Learning* (pp. 214-218; 204-206; 264-265). New York: CBS College Publishing.

Lawther, J. D. (1977). *The learning and performance of physical skills* (p. 128). (2nd ed.). Englewood Cliffs: Prentice-Hall.

Magill, R. (1980). *Motor Learning: Concepts and applications*. Dubuque, IA: William C. Brown Publishers.

Nelson, J. K. & Johnson, B. L. (1979). *Measurement of physical performance: Resource guide* (pp. 77-82). Minneapolis: Burgess Publishing Company.

Rothstein, A., Catelli, L., Dodds, P. & Manahan, J. (1981). *Motor learning: Basic stuff series I.* (pp. 75-78). Reston, VA: AAHPERD.

Schmidt, R. A. (1982). *Motor control and learning* (pp. 74-76). Champaign, IL: Human Kinetics Publishers.

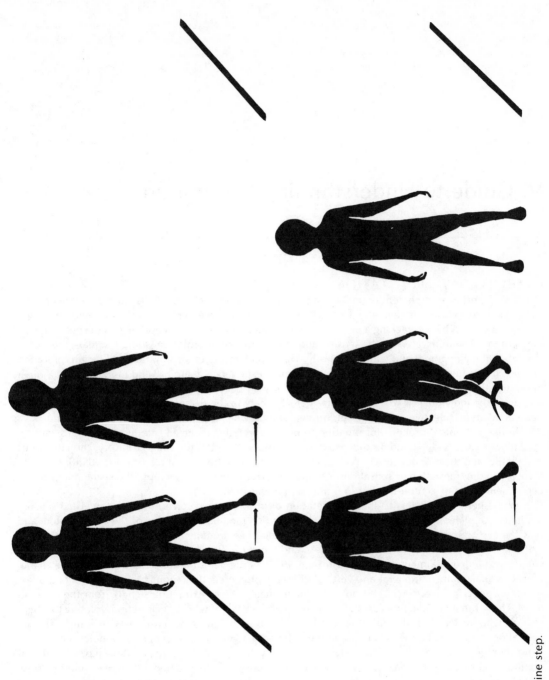

Figure 15. Slide and grapevine step.

23

V. Guide to Understanding Perception

OVERVIEW AND ORIENTATION

The importance of perception in learning and performance of motor skills cannot be overemphasized. Motor responses are dependent on it. The more efficient the perception the more effective will be the response. A batter tracking a pitched ball to be hit is employing perception as is the performer of a headstand. The term refers to the sensing and interpreting of information (stimuli, signals) present in the external environment and within the body. The apprehension of information and its interpretation are dependent upon a person's perceptual style, past experience, learning, and motivation. Although many signals may be sensed and interpreted similarly by people in general, perception is considered unique to the individual. It will differ from that of others to the extent that personal factors, such as perceptual style, selective attention, set, motivation, previous experience, and maturity differ.

In the perceptual process, information to be interpreted is received through the various sensory modalities of the body including the visual, the auditory, the olfactory, the gustatory, the cutaneous and tactile, and the proprioceptive. While in reality, a combination, if not all, of the modalities may be involved in the translation of sensations into meaning (formation of a percept), the visual and proprioceptor senses are of central interest in motor skill acquisition.

Visual perception refers to the interpretation of information received through the visual sensory modality. An in-depth understanding of visual perception requires knowledge of the visual system and how the eye operates to extract signals from the external environment. A detailed explanation of that system and its operation is beyond the purpose and scope of this Guide; however, the interested reader will find extended treatment of the topic in Sage (1977). Particular attention should be given to explanations of visual acuity, peripheral and vertical vision, depth perception, monocular movement parallax, retinal disparity, convergence, and optical flow in their roles of extracting signals from the environment. Those functions and processes of the eye are at the basis of teacher instructions relating to where to look, what to see, and what information should be used to determine path, speed, distance, and acceleration of objects. Further attention, in the detailed reading, should be paid to principles of the organization of perception, including the law of proximity, the law of similarity, relationship of figure and ground, closure, continuation of the good figure, and constancy. Instructional directives relating to selective attention, relevant cues, pattern recognition, and memory retrieval strategies have a basis in those principles. If the example, given above, of a batter tracking a ball were analyzed, it would be found to involve most of the functions and processes enumerated.

Proprioception, at times identified as kinesthetic perception, refers to information received through structures internal to the body. It is a sensing and interpreting of signals about position, movement, and effort of the body. A thorough understanding of perception based on proprioception, just as in visual perception, would require knowledge of such structures as joints, golgi tendon organs, pacinian corpuscles, ruffini endings, neuromuscular spindles including the alpha motor neurons and the gamma loop, and pertinent areas of the cerebrum and cerebellum. Discussion of those structures may be found in Schmidt (1982) and Sage (1977). Based on the operation of the proprioceptor sense are teaching instructions which emphasize the "feel" of movements. An analysis of the headstand, offered as an example above, would illustrate the information-giving operation of the proprioceptors as the individual attempts to strike a balance in accordance with his/her interpretation of the "feel" of the position.

The task of the teacher of motor skills is to translate what is known about perception into instructions and environmental arrangements which will facilitate the rapid extraction and interpretation of information. Literature pertaining to teaching practices is extensive. A summary of it would be prohibitive; however, based on findings and conclusions of some of the research in the area, a few suggestions may be made. They are:

1. Simplify the learning environment in such a way as to provide only the information most important to the motor act to be executed. Reduction of the amount of information to be perceived facilitates speed of perception. Learners, beginners particularly, can absorb only a limited amount of information. An example of simplifying the environment may be found in teaching batting: only a ball, pitcher, and backstop would be used rather than an opponent field of nine players.

2. Intensify crucial signals to be sensed and interpreted. Intensification aids selective attention and facilitates apprehension of the critical signal. A red ball against a white background can be seen much more readily than a white ball against the same background.

3. Tell the learner where to look, when, and for what to look. From among the many bits of information impinging upon the sensory modalities at any given moment in time, the learner must selectively attend to that which is most relevant to the task at hand. Instructions such as "keep your eye on the ball" or "watch the face of your opponent's racquet" help the learner to orient and selectively attend.

4. Create an expectancy set and teach the learner to anticipate the occurrence of a given bit of information. Based on long experience with a skill in a variety of movements, a performer will learn that the probability of occurrence of certain events is high. A ball thrown upward at a 45 degree angle will reach its height then fall at approximately the same angle. A learner can anticipate where the ball will land and move to that spot as the ball is projected into the air. Anticipation of an event not only results in reduced perceptual processing time, but also can reduce response time. Advanced performers have learned to perceptually anticipate and to arrive at closure based on minimal signals.

5. Teach beginners to recognize patterns of movement. Such recognition reduces the number of isolated bits of information to be sensed and interpreted; therefore, the span of apprehension will increase, while the time to perceive will be reduced. When, for example, the figure 8 weave is used to move a basketball down the floor, more meaning can be extracted from the total pattern than if each one of the players involved is seen alone. Observation without active participation can help learners to identify patterns. Advanced performers have learned to see and respond to a variety of configurations which may occur in motor skill situations.

6. Once beginners have moved beyond the very beginning stage, teach them to be sensitive to the feel of movements performed. In verbal instructions, the use of feeling words such as "*stretch* to the net on your follow through" may be helpful. Beginners tend to be visually oriented; however, for effective performance, proprioceptor signals in the form of feedback should be sensed and interpreted. Advanced performers have learned to perceive position, movement, and effort of their bodies. They make adjustments based on the meaning attached to the signals received.

KEY WORDS TO DEFINE OR DESCRIBE

Alpha Motor Neurons	Depth Perception	Golgi Tendon Organs
Anticipation	Effector Anticipation	Information Reduction
Apprehension	Expectancy Set	Law of Proximity
Attention	Feedback	Law of Similarity
Cerebellum	Field Dependence	Neuromuscular Spindle
Cerebrum	Field Independence	Perceptual Learning
Closure	Foveal Vision	Perceptual Organization
Continuation of Good Figure	Gamma Loop	Perceptual Speed

Pattern Recognition	Perceptual Style	Retinal Disparity
Percept	Peripheral Vision	Selective Attention
Perception	Proprioception	Set
Perceptual Anticipation	Propioceptors	Vertical Vision
Perceptual Apprehension	Receptor Anticipation	Visual Acuity

QUESTIONS FOR DISCUSSION

1. Diagram and study the visual system. Explain the reception of stimuli and the neural pathways over which the stimuli travel.

2. Diagram and study the organs of proprioception. Explain how stimuli are received and the neural pathways over which they travel.

3. How does the source of stimuli differ in visual and proprioceptive perception?

4. How do the sensory systems function together in the perceptual process? Does proprioception aid in visual perception? Does visual perception aid in proprioception?

5. What are the Gestalt principles of perception?

6. How is "attention" related to perception? What is "selective attention?"

7. Explain how motivation may affect perception?

8. How much time is required to form a percept?

9. How are we able to perceive depth? In what sports would depth perception be important?

10. Is the perception of speed of objects effective with all areas of the eye? Explain.

11. How are monocular, binocular, foveal, and peripheral vision related to visual perception?

12. How does anticipation speed up the process of perception?

13. Some investigators have attempted to identify the various perceptual abilities. They have listed perceptual speed, span of apprehension, depth perception, figure-ground, and perceptual flexibility. Determine the characteristics ascribed to these abilities, then analyze tennis and bowling to determine the need for these abilities.

14. If you wanted a middle distance runner to increase his/her speed and reduce time for the run, where would you instruct the runner to look? Why?

15. Based on the perceptual skills developed by advanced performers, explain how it is possible for a quarterback to throw a pass accurately to a receiver while the game is in process.

16. How would you reduce the amount of information to be perceived by a beginner learning to execute a free throw in basketball?

17. Discuss how observation of games in process may help beginners to develop their perceptual skills? Identify those skills.

18. Where would you instruct a performer to look when batting a softball to an opponent team in order to keep track of where all of the field players are located and what they are doing? Explain your answer.

19. How can you account for the fact that you are able to make "accurate" judgements about the size of a ball being thrown to you over a distance such as 2nd base to homeplate on a regulation baseball diamond?

20. What failure in visual perceptual abilities may account for:
    a. A basketball player not detecting a teammate cutting for a pass?
    b. The middle man in a fast break pattern in basketball not knowing where his teammates are located?
    c. Passing too late to a teammate moving toward an opening in field hockey?
    d. Moving to the net too late in badminton to compensate for a teammate backing up to return a high clear?
    e. Moving too late or too early to catch a flyball?

21. Can kinesthetic perception be improved through instruction and training? Explain.

22. Bowlers going after a strike often exclaim as the strike is missed, "I knew it the moment the ball left my hand." Explain how they were able to predict that the ball would not strike.

23. What is a kinesthetic figural aftereffect? How is it related to perception?

24. Are there some physical skills or sports skills which can be performed without the reception of visual stimuli? List as many as you can. Explain why the performer can execute these skills with consistency.

ACTIVITIES
1. Study the pictures or diagrams in the Recent Progress in Perception reference in your bibliography. Does your visual perception change as you continue to view the pictures? How? Explain why?

2. Study Figure 16. Describe what you see. What perceptual ability do the figures represent? Try drawing a similar type figure.

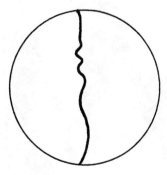

Figure 16. Ambiguous form.

3. Use a tachistoscope or a regular slide projector, flash a picture to a group of beginners of a number of dots (12 or more) on the screen for 5 seconds, how many dots did they see? Now flash a picture of a well known person on the screen for the same amount of time. Were they able to recognize and name the person? What perceptual ability is being exercised?

4. Working in partners facing. See Figure 14, Section IV of the Guide. Receive a ball thrown by your partner. How is the perceptual problem involved in "seeing" the ball like that applied in Activity (1) above?

5. Try the same acrivity as in (4) above but this time use a ball the same color as the surrounding wall, ex. white tennis ball against a white wall. How does the task of "seeing" change? Explain.

6. Work in partners with a lightweight ball (volleyball). Run side by side throwing and catching the ball while trying to keep your eyes focused ahead. Could you perform well?

7. Try activity (6) again, but this time, tape small cardboard blinders on the temple side of each eye. See Figure 17. Repeat the side by side run. Did your performance change? Explain.

Figure 17. Side by side run with eye blinders.

8. Work in partners facing. Use a tennis ball. Explain that one of the pair should close his eyes, the other will throw the ball at a 45° angle upward. The thrower immediately after releasing the ball will call out "open." The catcher should open his/her eyes and attempt to catch the ball. The thrower should observe the eye behaivor of the receiver closely. Describe it. Explain why the catch was successful even though the eyes were not focused on the ball all of the time.

9. Swing one bat, then use 3 or 4 bats to swing simultaneously as if batting a ball. Place all bats down except one. Swing that one immediately. Did you experience a change in the feel? Describe any change you felt. Explain the change?

10. Use a thick rubber band hooked over the thumbs of one partner and a 15" ruler. The partner with the band should close his eyes and stretch the band over his thumbs until it is 13" in length; then let the band contract. Immediately stretch the band again in an attempt to reach 13" in length. How accurate was he? Try a different length with eyes open on the first stretch, then close the eyes and try to repeat that stretch. How accurate was he? Which one was more accurate? Explain. What type of perception is being applied in this activity?

11. Place a soccer ball on a field about 70 yards away from a boundary line. Direct a beginner to determine how far the ball is away from the line. How accurate is the response? What perceptual principle does the activity represent?

12. Repeat (11) above with a tennis ball. Explain any difference in accuracy of response to (11) above and to the distance of the tennis ball.

13. Combine the forms shown in Figure 18 to complete any whole figure that occurs to you. Compare your completed form with the productions of your classmates. What form(s) was completed most frequently? Explain the result.

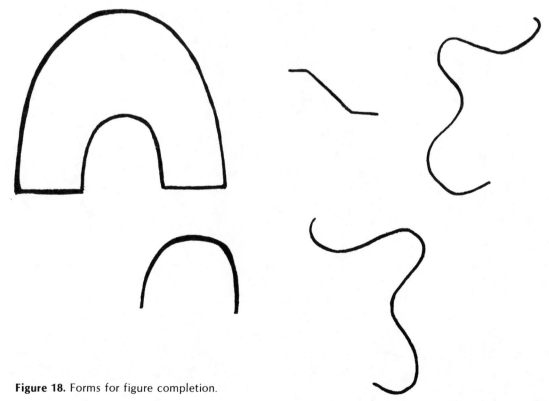

Figure 18. Forms for figure completion.

14. Grip a bat as if preparing to swing at a pitched ball. Try to become consciously aware of the weight of the bat first, then the pressure of the grip, the position of the elbows, position of shoulders, position of feet, position of hips. What type of perception does this exercise reperesent?

BIBLIOGRAPHY

Arend, S. (1980). Developing perceptual skills prior to motor performance. *Motor Skills: Theory into Practice, 4*(1), 11-17.

Attneave, F. (1976). Multistability in perception (pp. 143-152). *Recent progress in perception.* San Francisco: W. H. Freeman and Company.

Cockerill, I. M. & MacGillivary, W. W. (1981). *Vision and sport* (pp. 92-111). London: The Trinity Press.

Fitch, H. L., Tuller, B., & Turvey, M. T. (1982). The Bernstein perspective: Tuning of coordinative structures with special reference to perception. In J. A. S. Kelso (Ed.). *Human motor behavior: An introduction.* Hillsdale, NJ: Lawrence Erlbaum Associates.

Garry, R. & Kingsley, H. L. (1970). *The nature and conditions of learning* (pp. 370-398). Englewood Cliffs: Prentice-Hall.

Kerr, R. (1982). *Psychomotor learning* (pp. 127-139; 151-152). New York: Saunders College Pubishing.

Kimble, G. & Garmezy, N. (1968). *Principles of general psychology* (pp. 151-191; 221-258). New York: The Ronald Press.

Magill, R. (1980). *Motor learning: Concepts and applications* (pp. 67-91). Dubuque, IA: William C. Brown.

Pick, H. I. & Saltzman, E. (1978). *Modes of perceiving and processing information.* New York: John Wiley and Sons.

Rothstein, A., Catelli, L., Dodds, P. & Manahan, J. (1981). *Motor learning: Basic stuff series I* (pp. 8-10; 94-101). Reston, VA: American Alliance for Health, Physical Education, Recreation, and Dance.

Sage, G. (1977). *Introduction to motor behavior: A neuropsychological approach* (pp. 215-227; 231-233; 257-279). Reading, MA: Addison-Wesley Publishing Company.

Schmidt, R. A. (1982). *Motor control and learning* (pp. 129-136; 164-165). Champaign, IL: Human Kinetics Publishers.

Singer, R. N. (1980). *Motor learning and human performance* (pp. 229-234). New York: MacMillan Publishing Company.

Solley, C. M. & Murphy, G. (1960). *Development of the perceptual world* (pp. 153-287). New York: Basic Books.

VI. Guide to Understanding Motivation

OVERVIEW AND ORIENTATION

Motivation to learn or perform motor skills is of such importance that some writers have stated that skill is a multiplicative function of performance and motivation. It is important not only in aiding learning and performance, but also in a learner's selection of activities in which to engage.

In recognition of the significant role of motivation, teachers often pose questions such as: what motivates students?; why are some students motivated, while others are not?; how can the motivation of students be increased? There are no global answers to such questions; however, knowledge and understanding of theories pertaining to causes of behavior may provide a basis from which answers may be derived.

Theories of motivation purport to explain why people behave in given ways in various situations. Some base their explanations on psychological concepts of primary (biological and physiological) and secondary or acquired (learned) needs. Satisfaction of those needs becomes the reason for behavior. Other theories offer descriptions of the neurophysiological characteristics of motivated states which develop within the behaving individual. Such explanations are concerned with arousal and activation, and their effect on the individual.

Although universal agreement on definitions of the terms motivation and motive commonly used in theories is difficult to find, there is some acceptance of the interpretation that the term "motivation" refers to a general "energized" state which prepares the person to act or behave in some way, while "motive" relates to the direction that the behavior will take or the goal which will be sought. The strength of the "energized" state determines the vigor with which the goal-related behavior will occur.

The words "arousal" and "activation" are no less difficult to define than are motivation and motive. Some writers attempt to differentiate between the two words by citing the levels of the neurophysiological systems which are stimulated, others use the terms interchangeably. Neuroscientists refer to "arousal" as a phasic physiological response and "activation" as a tonic physiological readiness to respond. All agree that the reticular formation, located in the midbrain, which alerts and relays information to the cerebral cortex, is involved in the neurophysiological changes occurring within the individual under stimulating conditions. The "energized" state of the motivated individual is similar to, if not the same as, the conditions of "arousal" and "activation". It is to be noted that optimal stimulation facilitates perception, attention, and movement, all of which are important in the learning and performance of physical skills.

Although a learner/performer may be motivated to behave in given ways to satisfy needs and to reduce arousal/activation states without external inducement, often it becomes necessary for a teacher to apply motivational techniques to help to create a desire on the part of the student to learn and/or perform. Most of the external motivational approaches in common use are designed to appeal to acquired needs, such as acceptance, recognition, belonging, self-sufficiency, or mastery. Incentives of praise, reward, knowledge of results, pep talks, goal setting, and competition represent some of the techniques which may appeal to acquired needs. It must be recognized, however, that not all learners have the same motives thus techniques of motivation must be differentially applied. Such application is contingent upon understanding the student as a unique individual with given past experiences and characteristic ways of behaving and feeling under various conditions. The incentive value of activities, hence motivation to engage in them, is an individual decision.

Research on motivation, particularly on the arousal/activation response, has demonstrated that high levels of energization can have a detrimental effect if the learner is a beginner or is one who has a tendency toward stressful reactions in certain types of situations. The person who has developed proficiency in what is to be learned, and is not subject to undue tension, may be aided by high levels of motivation. An inverted "U," as in Figure 19, illustrates roughly how performance can be modified by levels of motivational states.

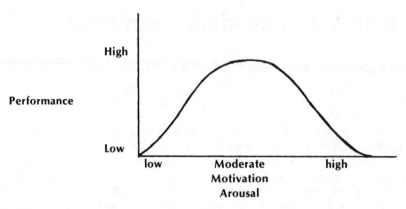

Figure 19. An inverted "U."

While response to stress may vary according to the individual and the situation, if the stress or tension factor and type of material to be learned are considered, as they are in Figure 20, the effect can be seen. Although the apparent linear relationship shown in Figure 20 is rarely found, the low stressful person does appear to be able to perform complex tasks under higher levels of motivation than does the high stressful individual.

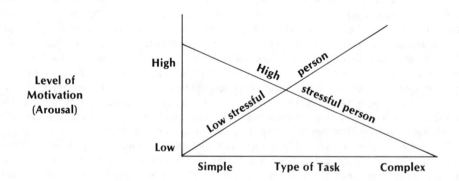

Figure 20. Hypothetical interaction of person, task, and motivation.

While research has not provided answers to the question of what constitutes optimal levels of motivation for the various types of activities involved in motor learning and performance, it has been demonstrated that very high levels of energization may result in loss of concentration, narrowed attention, and reduced fine coordination which can affect some types of motor skills. Balance type activities exemplify such skills. Other skills, such as those requiring explosive movements of short duration, may be executed most effectively by a performer who is highly aroused/activated.

In summary, teachers who have knowledge and understanding of motivation theory are in a position to select motivational techniques appropriate for the learner and the motor task to be mastered. Attention to individual differences is required to assure that each learner will attain a level of proficiency commensurate with his/her abilities and goals.

KEY WORDS TO DEFINE OR DESCRIBE

Acceptance	Goal	Perception
Achievement Motive	Goal Setting	Phasic
Acquired Need	Incentive	Physiological Need
Activation	Intrinsic Motivation	Physiological
Anxiety	Inverted "U" Hypothesis	Praise
Arousal	Knowledge of Results	Recognition
Attention	Level of Aspiration	Reticular Formation
Belonging	Mastery	Reward
Cerebral Cortex	Motivation	Self-sufficiency
Competence	Motive	Stress
Competition	Need	Stressor
Drive	Neurophysiological	Tonic
Extrinsic Motivation	Pep Talk	

QUESTIONS FOR DISCUSSION

1. Changing the intensity level of a stimulus or varying that level can affect the level of arousal/activation of the receiver of the stimulus. Discuss the effect that a teacher's voice (the stimulus) might have on the learner/performer (receiver) if it is changed from soft to loud or loud to soft.

2. Why would vigorous muscular activity tend to raise the level of arousal/activation?

3. Using the references, particularly Alderman (1974) and Drowatzky (1981), make a list of primary and acquired needs. What motivational techniques could you apply to appeal to those needs?

4. Identify several motivational techniques which you have used with learners and performers. Describe the effect on the behavior of the learner/performer.

5. Differentiate between intrinsic and extrinsic motivation. How could you help a learner/performer to develop intrinsic motivation?

6. Discuss the meaning of incentive. How may rewards, praise, knowledge of results, serve as incentives?

7. If a learner/performer is committed to the development of excellence in a well-liked activity, what incentives might be involved to support continuing effort to achieve that excellence?

8. The learner/performer who sets achievable personal goals may be more highly motivated to continue to apply effort to master a given skill than one who either has no goals or sets either too high or too low goals. To which of the motives, cited in the Overview and Orientation of this section of the Guide, does this theory of goal setting and level of aspiration apply? Explain.

9. At the beginning of learning a new skill, a teacher may provide, through demonstration or other means, an experience which acquaints the learner with what is to be learned before active instruction begins. Can such an approach be considered a motivational technique? Explain your answer.

10. Frequently, teachers observe that learner/performer, appear to become bored with using the same drills for skills being learned. What may the teacher do in such a situation? Why?

ACTIVITIES

1. Provide the members of a group of learners with blank sheets of paper. Direct each member to state the name of the activity in which he/she likes most to engage, then state the reason(s) why that activity has been named. Collect the papers and make a composite list of all of the reasons given. Try to relate those reasons to the list of motives cited in the Orientation and Overview of this section. What conclusion can you draw about individual motives?

2. Upon completion of activity (1) above, try to match the motives identified with motivational techniques.

3. Engage a group of learners in a quiet activity which is conducive to relaxation, such as lying on their backs on the floor with eyes closed for two or three minutes. Follow this immediately with a very vigorous running in place activity for one to two minutes. Ask learners to orally describe the feelings experienced under the two conditions.

4. Place a group of beginners in basketball in the formation shown in Figure 21 preparatory to introducing the chest pass:

Figure 21. Basketball pass formation.

After a demonstration and a few trials monitored by the teacher, instruct the learners to chest pass the ball as indicated by the dotted lines in the diagram. The goal is to complete *one* sequence of passes without dropping the ball or throwing it in such a way that the receiver cannot catch it easily. When that goal has been achieved, place Group A in competition with Group B. The winner of the competition will be the group which completes the succession of passes in the *least* amount of time with no errors. (A time limit of 45-60 seconds may be set). Observe the results. Comment on any change noted.

5. (A) Work in pairs. You will need a dart board and darts (a ball and target drawn on a wall may be used). Blindfold one partner, place him/her on a line about six feet away from target (12 feet if wall and ball are used). Instruct the blindfolded partner to throw five darts (balls) at the target, but do not provide any information on the outcome of the throws (knowledge of results). Record the score.

   (B) Repeat (A) above with the same blindfolded partner. On this set of trials, provide knowledge of results by telling the thrower that the darts (balls) did or did not hit the target. Record the score.

   (C) Repeat (A) above with the same blindfolded partner. After each throw, give knowledge of results by telling the partner exactly where the dart (ball) hit, and instruct as to how the aim should be adjusted for success. Record the score.

   (D) Upon completion of (C) above, remove the blindfold. Comment on any changes noted in performance. Explain your observation based on the role that knowledge of results may play in motivation. (This exercise may be tried using three different students, 1-A, 1-B, 1-C).

6. Use a mat marked off up to seven feet, on which a standing long jump may be performed. Work in pairs, with one of the pair as performer. Direct the performer to stand on edge of mat with back to the target. Ask the performer to estimate what the distance of the first jump will be. Direct the performer to jump. Measure the trial to the nearest inch. Determine the difference between what the performer estimated and the distance actually achieved. Repeat the process for five trials. Observe differences in distances attained. Record and observe any changes made by the performer, noting whether estimates increased or decreased. What motivational technique does this activity represent?[1]

CREDITS

[1]Adapted from: Cratty, B.J. and Hutton, R.S.: Experiments in Movement Behavior and Motor Learning. Lea & Febiger, Philadelphia, 1969.

BIBLIOGRAPHY

Alderman, R. B. (1974). *Psychological behavior in sport* (Chapter 8). Philadelphia: W. B. Saunders Company.

Cratty, B. J. (1973). *Teaching motor skills* (pp. 81-91). Englewood Cliffs: Prentice-Hall.

Cratty, B. J. & Hutton, R. S. (1969). *Experiments in movement behavior and motor learning* (p. 85). Philadelphia: Lea and Febiger.

Duffy, E. (1962). *Activation and behavior.* New York: John Wiley and Sons.

Duffy, E. (1972). Activation. In N. S. Greenfield & R. A. Sternbech (Eds.), *Handbook of Psychophysiology.* New York: Holt, Rinehart and Winston.

Drowatzky, J. N. (1981). *Motor learning: Principles and practices.* (2nd ed.). Minneapolis: Burgess Publishing Company.

Garry, R. & Kingsley, H. L. (1970). *The nature and conditions of learning* (pp. 168, 304-317). Englewood Cliffs: Prentice-Hall.

Kerr, R. (1982). *Psychomotor learning* (pp. 88, 93). New York: Saunders Publishing.

Landers, D. M. (1980). The arousal-performance relationship revisited. *Research Quarterly for Exercise and Sport, 51*(1), 77-90.

Lawther, J. D. (1977). *The learning and performance of physical skills* (pp. 169-191). (2nd ed.). Englewood Cliffs: Prentice-Hall.

Magill, R. (1980). *Motor learning: Concepts and applications* (pp. 211-222, 298-301). Dubuque, IA: William C. Brown.

Marteniuk, R. (1976). *Information processing in motor skills* (pp. 4, 192). New York: Holt, Rinehart and Winston.

Martens, R. (1974). Arousal and motor performance. In J. H. Wilmore (Ed.), *Exercise and Sport Science Reviews* (Vol. 2) New York: Academic Press.

Robb, M. (1972). *The dynamics of motor skill acquisition* (pp. 79-84). Englewood Cliffs: Prentice-Hall.

Stallings, L. (1982). *Motor learning: From theory to practice* (pp. 115-129). St. Louis: The C. V. Mosby Company.

VII. Guide to Understanding Task Analysis

OVERVIEW AND ORIENTATION

Knowledge of and skill in the classification and analysis of motor tasks constitute important tools for the effective teacher of motor skills. Well done classification and subsequent analysis not only can aid the teacher and learner/performer to develop an understanding of what behaviors, internal and external, are necessary to perform a motor act, but also can be instrumental in the selection of appropriate beginning points for the learner along with the identification of applicable practice conditions. An analysis may direct a teacher to apply whole, part, massed, or distributed practice in an unchanging or dynamic environment. Essential cues related to the type and timing of verbal instructions to be given by the teacher also might be provided. Effective observation of a performer executing a given skill is yet another valuable outcome of a careful analysis.

Since its inception, motor learning has reflected many approaches to the development and use of taxonomies and systems which provided a broad classification of skills according to some pattern of either movement or response. Gross, fine, discrete, serial, continuous, simple, and complex were terms used frequently to identify or categorize motor tasks. Among the early systems applied in study and application were those devised by Fitts (1962), Fleishman (1975), Gentile and colleagues (1975), Merrill (1972), and Poulton (1957). Those systems have viewed motor skills according to whether or not they were closed or open, self-paced or externally paced, simple or complex, or the same or different in behavior, behavior requirements, abilities or characteristics.

More recently, with the emphasis on information processing models of how learners/performers process information to produce a motor act interest in classification systems which relate to the components of those models has grown. Appearing in the literature are hierarchal models which reflect the hypothesized similarity between the human performer and the operation of a computer; schemes which classify motor tasks according to similarity of stimuli present, perceptual components, decision making functions, type and number of motor acts, feedback sources, types of feedback and timing, and approaches which combine information processing components with biomechanical and kinesiological factors.

Some of the systems are more practical than others for the teacher to use; however, the application of any of the broad systems will have limited effectiveness unless the completed analysis includes the "critical components" of the skill under consideration. Those components, defined as parts of a skill without which performers will be unsuccessful (Robb, 1972), form the content of what is to be taught at any given point in the learning of a motor skill. Currently, although biomechanics and kinesiology are beginning to generate important information about the motor act itself, much of the accuracy of an analysis will depend on the knowledge and the expertness of the teacher of the particular skill being analyzed.

KEY WORDS TO DEFINE OR DESCRIBE

Analysis	Biomechanics	Closed-loop Skills
Augmented Knowledge	Classification	Closed Loop
of Results	Closed Environment	Coherent

Components	Fine	Open-loop Skills
Continuous	Gross	Open Skill
Critical Components	Hierarchal	Perceptual Component
Decision Making	Internal Feedback	Self-paced
Discrete	Kinesiology	Serial
Executive Plan	Knowledge of Performance	Stimuli
External Feedback	Knowledge of Results	Subroutines
Externally Paced	Mixed Pace	Taxonomy
Feedback	Open Environment	

QUESTIONS FOR DISCUSSION

1. Define all of the terms in the terminology list, then select all terms which refer to task types. Discuss the similarities and differences in meaning. Do the same exercise with words referring to classification and to feedback.

2. Explain the meaning of "hierarchal organization" of a motor skill.

3. Differentiate between a closed environment, a closed skill, an open environment, and an open skill. Employing these terms, describe the skill of bowling.

4. How does analysis of a skill aid the teacher in the selection of a teaching strategy?

5. How may analysis of a skill aid the teacher in observation of a learner/performer?

6. Observation of a learner/performer frequently is followed by instructions and/or augmented knowledge of results provided by the teacher. How does the analysis of a skill assist the teacher in selecting appropriate instructions and/or augmented knowledge of results?

7. See Activity #3 in this section of the Guide. If you were applying that model to the analysis of motor tasks for children, how would it help you to decide where to begin instruction with children?

8. Find, in the reference list of this section, the name of Stallings. Study the model presented in the text on page 187, then draw a profile to describe archery and swimming. What does the profile suggest to you about practice conditions?

9. Find, in the reference list of this section, the name of Herkowitz. Study her models, then discuss how they may help a teacher to teach and evaluate progress in skill mastery.

ACTIVITIES

1. A. Image a performer ready to execute a basketball free throw, then using the contingency model, Figure 22, adapted from Singer (1980) below, locate the free throw in one of the blocks.

Environment

	Still	Moving
Still		
Performer		
Moving		

Figure 22. Contingency model.

Note: Singer Robert N.: The Psychomotor Domain: Movement Behavior. Lea & Febiger, Philadelphia, 1972.

B. From the terminology list, find the meaning of closed skill, open skill, self-paced, externally paced, and mixed pace skill; now offer a reason why you located the basketball free throw in the level chosen. Would you describe the skill as simple or complex? Why?

2. Work with a partner and a ball. One partner stands still and throws ball to the other member who is running. Using the contingency diagram in activity (1) above, classify the action for the partner standing still, then for the member who is running. Which of the partners is executing the most difficult of the two actions? Why?

3. Study the example of a hierarchal model in Figure 23, adapted from Marteniuk (1976), in which critical components of a tennis forehand have been identified:

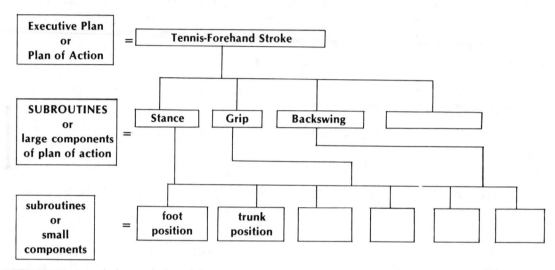

Figure 23. Sample hierarchal model.

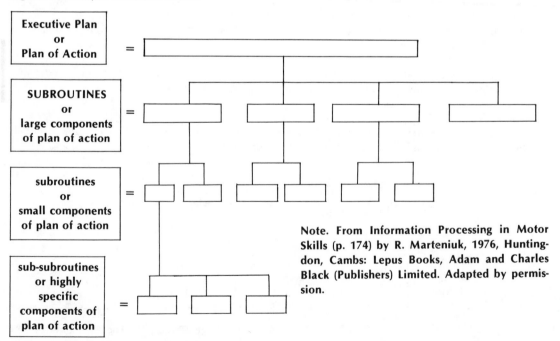

Note. From Information Processing in Motor Skills (p. 174) by R. Marteniuk, 1976, Huntingdon, Cambs: Lepus Books, Adam and Charles Black (Publishers) Limited. Adapted by permission.

Figure 24. Incomplete hierarchal model.

38

Now substitute in the model in Figure 24 a skill of your choice, identify the Executive Plan (plan of action), SUBROUTINES (large critical components), and subroutines (specific critical components). Try to extend the model vertically downward to show the most specific components which might represent abilities underlying subroutines, and SUBROUTINES.

4. A. Given the following subroutines, selected as critical components, of a one-hand, two-ball juggling skill, *underline* what you would select as key words to focus the attention of the learner on the components to be mastered; then analyze each subroutine as to whether it is a visual perceptual, kinesthetic perceptual, or motor component.

Type of Component	Subroutine	Action
	1.	Toss one ball upward with one hand, then catch it in the same hand.
	2.	Toss ball 3' upward with one hand and catch it.
	3.	Repeat (2) above, tossing ball in consistent pathway.
	4.	Repeat (2) and (3) above, now look at ball only at its height and move hand (without looking at it) in line with ball and catch it. Focus on height of ball.

B. How would an analysis such as 4-A above aid the teacher in the observation of a performer's execution of the juggling skill?

5. Applying an abbreviated form of an information processing model, such as was considered in Section II, Figure 2, of the Guide, try to locate each of the items in the following analysis of the components of a basketball free throw.

backboard; basket; ball; players on the lane; lane lines; officials; spectators; lighting; foveal vision; peripheral vision; vertical vision; type of shot to take; aiming; order of movements; outcome of the shot; how the shot felt; teachers' instructions based on outcome of shot.

BIBLIOGRAPHY

Arend, S. (1980). Developing the substrates of skilled movement. *Motor skills: Theory into practice, 4*(1), 3-10.

Billing, J. (1980). An overview of task complexity. *Motor skills: Theory into practice, 4*(1), 18-23.

Fitts, P.M. (1962). Factors in complex skill training. In R. Glaser (Ed.), *Training research and education.* Pittsburgh: University of Pittsburgh Press.

Fleishman, E.A. (1975). Toward a taxonomy of human performance. *American Psychologist, 30,* 1127-1149.

Gentile, A.M., Higgins, J.R., Miller, E.A. & Rossen, B.M. (1975). The structure of motor tasks. *Mouvement 7.* Actes 7e symposium en apprentisage psycho-moteur et psychologie du sport. Quebec City.

Herkowitz, J. (1978). Developmental task analysis: The design of movement experiences and evaluation of motor development status. In M. Ridenour (Ed.), *Motor development: Issues and applications.* Princeton, NJ: Princeton Book Company.

Higgins, J.R. (1977). *Human movement: An integrated approach* (pp. 12-27). St. Louis: The C. V. Mosby Company.

Kerr, R. (1982). *Psychomotor learning* (pp. 9-17). New York: Saunders College Publishing.

Magill, R.A. (1980). *Motor learning: Concepts and application* (pp. 18-21). Dubuque, IA: William C. Brown.

Marteniuk, R. (1976). *Information processing in motor skills* (pp. 25, 145). New York: Holt, Rinehart, and Winston.

Merrill, M.D. (1972). Taxonomies, classifications, and theory. In R.N. Singer (Ed.), *The psychomotor domain: Movement behavior.* Philadelphia: Lea and Febiger.

Poulton, E.C. (1970). On prediction in skilled movements. In D. Legge (Ed.), Baltimore: Penguin Books.

Robb, M. (1972). *Dynamics of motor skill acquisition* (pp. 116-132; 135-150). Englewood Cliffs: Prentice-Hall.

Rothstein, A., Catelli, L., Dodds, P. & Manahan, J. (1981). *Motor learning: Basic stuff series I* (chapter II). Reston, Virginia: American Alliance for Health, Physical Education, Recreation, and Dance.

Schmidt, R.A. (1982). *Motor control and learning* (pp. 51-55). Champaign, IL: Human Kinetics Publishers.

Singer, R.N. (1980). *Motor learning and human performance* (pp. 13-22) (3rd ed.). New York: MacMillan Publishing Company.

Spaeth-Arnold, R.K. (1980). Developing sport skills: A dynamic interplay of task, learner, and teacher. *Motor skills: Theory into practice* (Monograph 2).

Stallings, L.M. (1982). *Motor learning: From theory to practice* (pp. 182-193). St. Louis: The C. V. Mosby Company.

VIII. Guide to Understanding Instructions: Demonstration and Verbal Guidance

OVERVIEW AND ORIENTATION

Instructions to introduce learners to a task and to guide responses made are among the most important preparations for a teacher to make. The selection and effective application of the form of instruction depend on the level of the learner, the type of motor task, and the environment in which performance takes place. Ideally, instructions should be developed to involve as many as possible of the sensory modalities of the learner. Demonstrations and verbalizations often are employed to introduce, describe, reinforce, and correct motor responses involved in the acquisition of motor skills. At times, manual and mechanical guidance are applied; however, visual guidance in the form of demonstration and auditory guidance in the form of verbalizations appear to have wide usage.

At the initial stage of learning, it is important to establish for the learner an overall "gross framework idea" (Lawther, 1977, p. 91) of what is to be mastered. Since beginners and children appear to rely more on the visual modality than on other sensory modalities, the demonstration, when executed properly, can facilitate learning. Once the goal of a movement is imaged, the learner can begin to put together movements to arrive at that goal. In the presentation of a "gross framework idea," it is important to emphasize only the most critical components. Although demonstrations most often are provided by the teacher, in some instances a peer of the learner may present the model. Films, film loops, videotapes and other similar visuals are additional ways of providing images. In all cases care should be taken to include models which are not so complex or so removed from the learner's level that he/she becomes confused by detail or is unable to identify with the performance. When verbal explanation accompany demonstrations, verbalizations should be well chosen and limited to essential points so as not to interfere with the idea of the goal to be achieved. The beginner, initially attempting to reach the goal, may only approximate the desired result; however, with further practice, accompanied by reinforcing and corrective instructions from the teacher, the learner can realize the intended goal with some skillfulness.

While conclusions about the usefulness of demonstrations to performers who have moved beyond a beginning stage are not definitive, it does appear that until a performer has reached a highly proficient level, the technique can be employed successfully to show specific critical details necessary to refine a skill. With the advancement of instrumentation in biomechanics, kinetic and kinematic models are being developed to provide individualized instruction for advanced performers.

Verbalization probably is the most frequently used type of instruction. Words can be instrumental in describing the general idea of some skills. They are useful to focus the learner's attention on critical components and to offer words or phrases toned to represent the feel of a movement. Some writers state that verbal explanation may be the quickest way to teach a skill if performers have associated certain verbalizations with given movements. Research, although limited, has concluded that the application of verbal labels relevant to a movement facilitates the learning of that movement (Shea, 1977). Some writers, Cratty (1973) for example, make the point that words which a performer employs in the execution of a movement are self-instructing. Teachers may find that the inclusion of such verbalizations in their instructions is effective.

40

Answers to questions relating to the content, timing, and extent of verbal instructions should take into account the type of skill, and the level of the performer. Although some relatively simple skills can be described well in words, many complex ones defy descriptive words and phrases. In the latter case verbalizations may be effective in establishing the "gross framework idea", however, other modes of instruction, demonstration for example, might have to be added to provide a visual image of movements indescribable in words. Consideration of the level of proficiency of a performer leads to general agreement among writers that the peformer who is above the beginning level is apt to profit more from verbal instruction than a beginner. Experience with a skill being taught increases the vocabulary of the performer. Words descriptive of an action to be taken can be understood and interpreted. Verbal instructions should be within the range of understanding of the receiver. Children and beginners can be guided as well as the advanced learner if words appropriate to their level are selected. Frequently, instructions which associate movements with previously encountered experiences are helpful because they provide a label which permits cognitive rehearsal. For example, in teaching a forward roll, instructions directing the learner to "make the body round like a ball" are effective in eliciting an appropriate movement from children and beginners. "Tuck your chin to your chest" may be all that is needed for the advanced learner.

The timing for the giving of instructions to beginners is crucial. Verbalizations should be planned to occur before and/or after the execution of a movement so as not to distract attention of the learner from the act being performed. Information processing theory testing has demonstrated that there are limitations to the number of stimuli to which an individual can attend simultaneously. Instructions may be considered as stimuli in the learner's environment. While timing of verbalizations is still important with the advanced performer, through experience with the skill being performed that performer has learned what is critical to attend to and what is not. Introductory responses, whether provided through verbalization, demonstration, or both should be timed in such a way as to permit the learner to execute the described movement without delay. The longer the period of time between the presentation of a "gross framework idea" and a learner's attempt to attain the goal described, the less accurate the approximation will be.

While instructions usually are associated with the initiation of learning, they continue to be involved in the form of reinforcement and corrections after the learner responds. The terms knowledge of results (K-R) and knowledge of performance (K-P) describe the directions afforded to a learner after movement has occurred. The former term relates to information received about the achievement of the goal of the movement while the latter describes knowledge about the execution of the movement. Both of those sources of information, sometimes referred to as extrinsic, are available to the performer with a teacher's involvement; however, if the teacher, through verbalization, demonstration, or both, offers information in addition to that already available to the learner, the terms augmented knowledge of results (AKR) and augmented knowledge of performance (AKP) are used. It is within AKR and AKP that instructions as interpreted here are found. The type, amount, and timing of those forms of extrinsic feedback are contingent upon the purpose to be served and the performer's level of proficiency.

Although general AKR and AKP have been observed to serve a motivational role, most investigations emphasize the importance of the instructional role of these two forms of information. To serve as information to the learner, verbalizations and/or demonstrations given as AKR and/or AKP should be specific enough to the movement being performed to provide a basis for improvement in the response. It is not enough for a teacher to say, for example, "good try" or "well done", rather it would be more effective to say "the goal was missed, try to begin the movement from the shoulder on your next swing." The exactness of the detail would depend on the level of the performer. Advanced performers appear to profit more from specifics than do children and beginners.

The timing of the AKR and AKP, although frequently studied, has not been determined conclusively. Some investigators have found that delaying the augmented information, especially in complex skills, to afford the performer time to experience his/her own K-R and K-P is beneficial; others have concluded that manipulation of the timing of AKR and AKP makes little difference. For a full discussion of the topic, Schmidt (1982, p. 257) should be consulted.

While examination of the literature may reveal many points of disagreement as to content, extent, and timing of instructions designated as augmented knowledge of results and augmented knowledge of performance, agreement will be found on the critical role served. Learning and performance are facilitated by appropriate extrinsic feedback provided by the teacher.

KEY WORDS TO DEFINE OR DESCRIBE

AKP	Critical Components	Kinesthetic
AKR	Extrinsic Feedback	Kinetic
Attention	Feedback	Knowledge of Performance
Auditory Mode	Gross Framework Idea	Knowledge of Results
Augmented Knowledge of	Information Processing	Labeling
Performance	Intrinsic Feedback	Motivation
Augmented Knowledge of	K-P	Sensory Modalities
Results	K-R	Stimuli
Biomechanics	Kinematic	Visual Mode

QUESTIONS FOR DISCUSSION

1. To establish a "gross framework idea" of badminton, a teacher, using all of the strokes found in the game, demonstrates how the game is played; then, without further instructions directs a learner to execute a service stroke. Comment on the effectiveness of the demonstration. Explain the changes you might make to introduce the stroke. State the reasons for the changes.

2. Discuss the advantages and disadvantages of visual aids, such as films, filmstrips, and videotapes to establish a "gross framework idea." How may a teacher remove some of the disadvantages?

3. Why is it important for a learner to try a movement immediately following a verbal description or demonstration of a skill?

4. Discuss the advantages and disadvantages of a demonstration performed by the teacher. How may the teacher avoid some of the disadvantages?

5. Why should verbal instructions not be provided while a learner is in the process of performing a movement which he/she is just beginning to learn?

6. How would you verbally describe a cartwheel, for example, to children? to beginners? to advanced learners? Explain the changes which you might make for the three different types of learners.

7. What is the difference between intrinsic and extrinsic feedback?

8. At what stage(s) of learning a new skill are augmented knowledge of results and performance appropriate to use? Explain your answer.

9. Which of the two types of augmented extrinsic feedback (AKR or AKP) would be most effective to apply if a learner is trying to perfect a skill? Explain your answer.

10. With what types of learners is manual guidance appropriate to use?

11. What are the advantages and disadvantages of using manual guidance in instruction?

ACTIVITIES

1. Work in partners. One of the pair serves as teacher, the other as learner. Select a "new skill," one with which the learner has had *little* or *no* experience. Introduce that skill with a generalized verbal description. After one explanation, have the learner execute the skill as described. Observe the response and answer the following questions: Did the learner get the idea of the skill? How many components of the skill were executed? Did the learner use self-instructions? Repeat the procedure with another learner, but use words in the verbal description which are within the vocabulary level of the learner, are descriptive of the feeling of the action, and point up only the most critical components of the movement. Observe the response and answer the questions above. Which learner appeared to respond best?

2. Prepare a set of instructions for the introduction of the forward roll to a group of high school students, then adjust the instructions for presentation to children in the primary grades. Compare the two sets of instructions. How do they differ? Evaluate their potential effectiveness with students at the two different grade levels.

3. Stand facing a group of learners to whom you will teach the following calisthenic:

> Trunk bending forward and sideward;
> Beginning forward, then left, then right;
> Repeat the movement four times consecutively
>   forward, four times to the left, four times
>   to the right;

Demonstrate the movements counting: *Forward,* 2, 3, 4; *Left,* 2, 3, 4; *Right,* 2, 3, 4, while you perform them in that order. On signal "Ready-Begin," have learners perform the movements. Observe the accuracy with which they duplicate the directions of the movements demonstrated.

Repeat the procedure, but execute the demonstration with your back to the group. Observe the response. Comment on the effectiveness of the two demonstrations in eliciting the desired response from the learners.

4. Figure 25 shows a performer rolling a ball down the forearm to project it into the air by straightening the arm just as the ball rolls to elbow joint (see also Activity 2, Section X). Demonstrate this novel skill to a learner, but do not verbalize the movements. Direct the learner to execute the skill. Ask the learner to describe in words what he/she actually did. Was the learner successful in performing the skill? Were the words of the learner the same as the ones you would have used?

Figure 25. A novel skill.

5. Blindfold a learner and stand him/her in front of a blackboard. Place a piece of chalk in his/her hand. Direct the learner to draw a horizontal line 14 inches long on the blackboard. Measure the result with a ruler. Tell the still blindfolded learner the number of inches that the drawn line is more or less than the standard set. Ask the learner to draw another line. Measure as before. Comment on the results. What type of instructions does this exercise involve?

6. Try (5) above but manually guide the first trial of the learner. Compare results with (5).

7. Prepare a set of instructions designed to impart a "gross framework idea" to children who are being introduced to the concept of space and the use of the body in that space. How would those instructions differ from those used to direct the movement of the body in a specific way through space? Explain how demonstration, augmented knowledge of results and performance would be applied.

BIBLIOGRAPHY

Bird, A.M. & Rikli, R.A. (1983). Observational learning and practice variability. *Research Quarterly for Exercise and Sport, 54*(1), 1-4.

Cratty, B.J. (1973). *The teaching of physical skills* (pp. 55-68). Englewood Cliffs: Prentice-Hall.

Drowatzky, J.N. (1981). *Motor learning: Principles and practices* (2nd ed.) (pp. 261-264). Minneapolis: Burgess Publishing Company.

Felz, D.L. (1982). Effects of age and number of demonstrations on modeling of form and performance. *Research Quarterly for Exercise and Sport, 53*(4), 291-296.

Garry, R. & Kingsley, H. *The nature and conditions of learning* (3rd ed.) (pp. 355-359). Englewood Cliffs: Prentice-Hall.

Gentile, A.M. (1972). A working model of skill acquisition with application to teaching. *Quest, 17,* 3-23.

Holding, D.H. (1970). Knowledge of results. In D. Legge (Ed.), *Skills*. Baltimore: Penguin Books.

Lawther, J.D. (1977). *The learning and performance of physical skills* (2nd ed.) (pp. 89-98; 124-126). Englewood Cliffs: Prentice-Hall.

Lockhart, A. (1966). Communicating with the learner. *Quest, 6,* 57-67.

Logsdon, B.J. & Barrett, K.R. (1969). *Teacher's manual: Ready? Set . . . go*. Bloomington, IN: National Instructional Television.

Magill, R.A. (1980). *Motor learning: Concepts and applications* (pp. 328-330). Dubuque, IA: William C. Brown.

Newell, K. (1981). Skill learning. In D.H. Holding (Ed.) *Human skills*. New York: John Wiley and Sons.

Robb, M. (1972). *The dynamics of motor skill acquisition* (pp. 58-59; 106-111). Englewood Cliffs: Prentice-Hall.

Schmidt, R.A. (1982). *Motor control and learning* (pp. 476-481; 527-562). Champaign, ILL: Human Kinetics Publishers.

Shea, J.B. (1977). Effects of labeling on motor short-term memory. *Journal of Experimental Psychology, 3,* 92-99).

Snellgrove, L. (1981). Knowledge of results. In L.T. Benjamin, Jr. & K.D. Lowman (Eds.), *Activities Handbook for the Teaching of Psychology*. Washington, DC: American Psychological Association.

Thomas, J.R. (1980). Acquisition of motor skills: Information processing differences between children and adults. *Research Quarterly for Exercise and Sport, 51*(1), 158-173.

Weiss, M.R. (1982). Developmental modeling. *Journal of Physical Education, Recreation, and Dance, 53*(9), 49-50; 67.

IX. Guide to Understanding Retention of Motor Skills

OVERVIEW AND ORIENTATION

One of the outcomes of learning is assumed to be retention of what has been learned. If one remembers past learning, one is said to have retained the information. Retention, then, refers to what is remembered. "It is the persistence of learning over periods of no practice" (Lawther, 1977, p. 147). Long term retention enables a learner, through recall and recognition processes, to use information in the future without the necessity for relearning it.

Just as the remembering of verbal learning is the focus of disciplines involving verbal skills, the retention of motor skills is the concern of motor learning. Although some investigations have attempted to differentiate between verbal and motor retention, others have concluded that there is no difference between the two.

Studies involving motor skills have determined that retention is a function of the meaningfulness of a task, the nature of the task, and the degree of original learning. Meaningfulness permits the learner to perceive the relationship existing among the parts of the task. In addition, association with past experiences are identified. Meaningfulness may be enhanced when the learner understands the ultimate goal of a task to be achieved. Continuous type skills such as swimming and those in which the parts are highly integrated appear to be remembered better than serial and discrete type motor tasks. Skills which have been learned and practiced beyond one or a few correct executions are said to be overlearned. Overlearning favors retention.

As a result of early and current investigations of the topic, teachers involved with skill acquisition have been provided with several guidelines for developing practice conditions to facilitate retention. Those guidelines take into account the memory processes of short term sensory storage, short term memory, and long term memory. While it is very important to understand the role and the relationship of those processes, discussion of them is beyond the scope of this section. Details may be found in Marteniuk (1976), Magill (1980), and Schmidt (1981) listed in the bibliography. Within the summary of guidelines that follows, the practice condition recommended is related, when possible, to the processes on which it is based. Effective practice conditions include:

1. Helping the learner to find meaningfulness in the task to be learned. Meaningfulness can be enhanced by establishing an image of the goal to be achieved, teaching for transfer through association, and providing motivating conditions to aid the learner to maintain effort in practice.

2. Helping the learner to develop strategies to facilitate short term sensory storage and short term memory. Those strategies include emphasis on selective attention to relevant information, chunking of information, and mental rehearsal. Labelling and cueing are useful ways of holding important information in short term storage. Without appropriate strategies, information stored in the sensory systems and in short term memory may fade within a span of less than one to sixty seconds. Actions taken by learners during that brief amount of time favor short term storage and eventual passage of information to long term memory.

45

3. Providing practice time to permit at least 50% more trials (overlearning) than were executed to achieve the first successful attempts.

4. Analyzing the nature of the task to determine the appropriate methods to use in teaching. Although long term retention may not be a function of method, early learning is affected; therefore, decisions about the application of massed or distributed and whole or part approaches are of some importance. Progressive part methods may be helpful particularly in mastering parts of a serial skill; while whole approaches are useful with those skills in which the parts are highly integrated.

5. Spacing practice periods in such a way that the amount of time between practices (referred to as "retention intervals") does not interfere with memory processes.

6. Arranging retention interval activity to reduce interference with the task being learned. Although research conclusions vary, the possibility exists that interval activities which interfere with information processing capacity or structures of the body required by the movement weaken retention. Both Stelmach (1974) and Laabs and Simmons (1981) summarize and discuss the research on motor memory.

7. Providing variety in the practice of a skill, particularly open type skills. Varied practice appears to facilitate the formation of schemas. Schemas refer to generalized representations or rules of relationship between past outcomes produced by the learner and what the learner actually did (Schmidt, 1981, p. 493). It is thought that long term memory consists of those types of representations.

KEY WORDS TO DEFINE OR DESCRIBE

Attention	Long Term Motor Memory	Retention
Chunking	(LTMM)	Retention Interval
Closed Skills	Memory	Schema
Continuous Skills	Mental Rehearsal	Serial Skills
Cueing	Open Skills	Short Term Memory (STM)
Discrete Skills	Overlearning	Short Term Motor Memory
Labelling	Recall	(STMM)
Long Term Memory (LTM)	Recognition	Short Term Sensory Storage
		(SSS)

QUESTIONS FOR DISCUSSION

1. What is the difference between retention and foregetting?

2. Discuss the similarities and differences between verbal and motor skill retention.

3. What is the difference between recall and recognition memory?

4. How is "recognition" described or defined in motor memory?

5. Retention may be adversely affected by retroactive or proactive inhibition. What do the terms mean? Why does interference with what is being learned take place?

6. Why should a teacher direct learners to practice a skill as soon as possible after it has been demonstrated or described?

7. Why is it essential for a learner to develop "strategies" for holding information in short term memory?

8. At any moment in time, we are bombarded by information (stimuli) through our sensory modalities. Most of that information, if not all, is lost within 250 milliseconds to one second. How does selective attention help us to retain some of that information?

9. What strategies have been found useful in the successful retrieval of information from long term memory?

10. Once well learned, motor skills are retained for many years. What are some of the reasons given for that long term retention?

11. The sequence of movements in a motor skill is more resistant to forgetting than the timing of those movements. What are some of the explanations of the observed difference in retention?

12. Why are continuous skills retained better than discrete skills?

13. Define or describe the phrase "retention interval." Discuss its significance with respect to the memory processes?

14. What type of activity, if any, should be carried out during retention intervals? Explain.

15. Meaningful information is remembered longer than non-meaningful information. What explanations are given for the longer retention of meaningful material?

16. Is the information stored in long term memory an exact representation of that which has been learned? Explain.

17. Some investigators indicate that manual manipulation, used as an instructional technique, may interfere with motor memory. Based on your understanding of "recognition" memory for motor movements, explain why such an instructional technique might interfere with memory.

ACTIVITIES

1. Orally present a set of digits to a group, for example, 5-1-3-6-7-2-9-8. Instruct the group to listen carefully because members will try to repeat the digits exactly as you say them. Present the digits in a monotone with a brief pause between each digit. When completed, ask the group to repeat the digits. Observe the response. Account for the inaccuracies which occurred.

2. Repeat (1) above, but this time, when you orally present the digits, group them as: 513-672-98. Observe the response. Compare the response with (1) above. Which of the two exercises would you expect to have fewer inaccuracies? Why?

3. Behind a screen, draw Figure 26 on the blackboard. Instruct students that they will have five seconds to study the figure when you raise the screen. After five seconds the screen will be lowered, and students will try to reproduce the figure using pencil and paper. Observe the response. How would you account for the results of the reproductions?

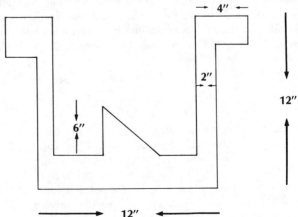

Figure 26. Irregular form.

4. Cut a pattern for the two forms in Figure 27 out of cardboard. Place four pieces of paper, and a pencil on a table. Blindfold a student seated at the table with pencil in hand and two pieces of paper in front of him/her within normal writing range. Place form A in front of him/her on one of the pieces of paper. Have the student trace the form by feeling its edges, then direct him/her to reproduce it with the pencil. Follow the same procedure with form B. Which of the two figures was reproduced with greater accuracy? Why?

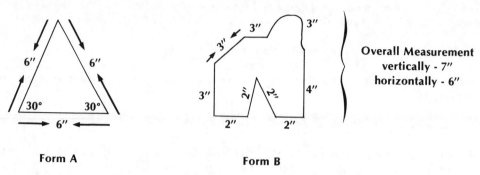

Form A   **Form B**

Figure 27. Forms with blindfold.

5. Repeat (4) above with another student, but this time, present form B, then form A, followed immediately by form B again. (On the second presentation of form B, do not permit the student to retrace the figure by feeling with a finger — the student should reproduce it immediately on paper with pencil.) Observe the response. Account for the result in the reproduction of form B.

6. Activity (4) and (5) above may be repeated without a blindfold. Once the forms have been traced by feeling with the fingers, remove them from sight and have the student reproduce them on paper with pencil. Account for the results obtained under the three different conditions posed by (4) and (5) above in this exercise.

7. Direct students to close their eyes, and, keeping the elbow straight, raise the non-preferred arm from the side to form a 90-degree angle at the shoulder between the upper body and the neck. Observe the response; then instruct them to relax the arm, letting it fall to the side. With eyes still closed, ask them to image the face of a clock, then raise the arm so that the fingers point to either 9:00 or 3:00 on that clock. Observe the accuracy of the response. Which of the two 90-degree angles formed was most accurate? Why?

8. Present a four step Schottische, as described below, by demonstration *only* to one half of a group, with the other half of group closing eyes. When finished with the demonstration, send the first half of the group to another area to practice. Now, demonstrate the same step to the second half of the group, and add words descriptive of the pattern and in the rhythm of the pattern. During its practice, the second group should be told to repeat the descriptive phrases to themselves silently. Each group should practice no more than five minutes. Immediately following practice, bring the groups together and have each half show what has been achieved. Which group would you expect to perform the step the best? Why?

The Four Step Schottische

Time	"Slide	—	Cut	—	Leap	—	Hop"
Pattern 4/4	1		2		3		4
Description	Left foot slides diagonally forward with weight on it		quickly close right foot to left; transfer weight to right foot, left foot swings forward and upward		transfer weight to left foot quickly		hop on left foot

48

Repeat pattern beginning right foot; continue repeating left, then right until eight whole steps have been completed.

9. Given the main components of an overhead clear in badminton: (a) the grip, (b) the stance, (c) the backward swing of the recquet, (d) the forward swing of the racquet, (e) point of contact with the shuttlecock, and (f) followthrough. If all of the details cannot be attended to by learners when a demonstration of the stroke is presented and cannot be held in the first stages of the memory processes very long, how could you "chunk" the details of the movements to overcome the short time span of the memory processes? Describe and demonstrate the approach you would use. Explain how that approach would facilitate storage. Would there be any disadvantages to the approach used? Explain.

10. Refer to the novel skill in Figure 28. Have students practice that skill until they can reach the criterion of five out of five successful catches in as many ten-second trials as they need before the criterion of five out of five is reached. Ask the students to continue the practice until they have taken one-half of their original trials. (Ex. if a student has eight trials to arrive at criterion, then practice four more trials.) Observe the consistency with which five out of five successes are made. Two days later (without practice in between), ask them to repeat the skill. Were all able to achieve five out of five successes on the first trial after the two days without practice? Use the formula to determine if overlearning resulted in good retention. The formula is OL-RL/OL = "Savings Score," in which OL = the number of trials originally taken to reach the criterion of five out of five successes, and RL = the number of trials after two days of practice to reach the criterion. The savings score will provide a measure of retention based on overlearning.

Figure 28. Novel skill.

BIBLIOGRAPHY

Cratty, B.J. (1973). *Teaching motor skills* (pp. 121-132). Englewood Cliffs: Prentice-Hall.

Kerr, P. (1982). *Psychomotor learning* (pp. 99-115). New York: Saunders College Publishing.

Laabs, G.J. & Simmons, R.W. (1981). Motor memory. In D.H. Holding (Ed.), *Human skills.* New York: John Wiley and Sons.

Lawther, J.D. (1977). *The learning and performance of physical skills* (2nd ed.) (pp. 147-149). Englewood Cliffs: Prentice-Hall.

Magill, R. (1980). *Motor learning: Concepts and applications* (pp. 126-141). Dubuque, IA: William C. Brown.

Marteniuk, R. (1976). *Information processing in motor skills* (pp. 8-9; 85-97). New York: Holt, Rinehart, and Winston.

Minehan, N.M. (1971). *Experiments on a shoestring* (pp. 57; 62-63). Unpublished Paper, Department of Psychology, University of Illinois.

Schmidt, R.A. (1981). *Motor control and learning* (pp. 113-124; 613-616; 618-628). Champaign, ILL: Human Kinetics Publlishers.

Singer, R.N. (1982). *The learning of motor skills* (pp. 173-184). New York: MacMillan Publishing Company.

Stelmach, G. (1974). Retention of motor skills. In J.H. Wilmore (Ed.), *Exercise and sport science reviews* (Vol. 2). New York: Academic Press.

X. Guide to Understanding Transfer

OVERVIEW AND ORIENTATION

The introduction and instructional approach to motor skill acquisition selected by teachers to facilitate learning frequently reflect a dependence upon relationships which might exist between two or more skills. The effect of the relationship on the learning of either of the skills is referred to as transfer.

Transfer is defined as the influence of one task on the learning of another. The influence may be proactive or retroactive. Proactive transfer involves the effect of a previously learned task on a new task; while a retroactive result describes the influence of a new task on one which has been learned already. When the mastery of one task aids in the learning of another one, there is positive transfer. Negative transfer occurs if a learned task creates difficulty in the mastery of another. Zero transfer is observed in those instances where one skill has no effect, positively or negatively, on another one.

Proactive transfer appears often in the teaching of motor skills. Lead-up activities designed to introduce learners to simplified forms similar to complex skills are in common use. Often, a basis for similarity is established by employing principles of body and object movement derived from body mechanics, kinesiology, and physics. Currently, attention is being focused on information processing components which may resemble each other in different skills. The components of perception, decision making, motor planning, and feedback are under investigation to determine their role in transfer.

Answers to questions about the most effective instructional approach to employ to assure effective transfer are not arrived at easily. The literature and research pertaining to the influence of previous learning on new learning is both extensive and complex. Some of the complexity stems from the several theoretical explanations of how and under what conditions different types of transfer may take place. Probably, the most frequently cited theories are identical elements, generalization (transfer by principles) and transposition (transfer by relationship). No one of those theories alone has offered an explanation adequate enough to account for what the learner transfers, nor for how and under what instructional conditions the process takes place. Explanations of the transfer between two tasks have included the influence of problem solving skills, learning how to learn, principles of relationships, and identical elements.

Research based on the theories cited has pointed up the need to consider the results in accordance with the unique characteristics and experiences of the learner. In addition, some writers emphasize the roles that method of instruction and type of task play. Whether or not whole to part, or part to whole approaches are used with simple or complex tasks may make a difference in transfer results. Given the characteristics and experiences of the learners along with the type of task and approach to teaching, it becomes apparent that the bases for transfer may not be the same for one learner as they are for another.

Whether or not the positive transfer expected by teachers, employing the common practices cited above, takes place is uncertain. In fact, one school of learning theory states that direct, specific instruction is preferred over instruction which depends upon establishing resemblance between and among tasks. In motor learning, there are those scholars who have concluded that motor skills are specific; therefore, little, if any, transfer can be anticipated to take place. They, too, recommend direct and specific teaching of a skill. Contrary to the beliefs held about specificity, there is some evidence to suggest that experiences in a wide variety of movement patterns which underly skills requiring similar patterns do have transfer value.

Despite the continuing specificity question, practitioners and researchers in motor learning maintain a high level of interest in the transfer potential of verbalizations to motor acts, limb to limb movements (bilateral transfer), skill to skill relationships, abilities to skill, and simple motor tasks to complex tasks.

The study of transfer has made apparent the need to take many factors into consideration. Although no explanations have been found adequate enough to account for the what and how of transfer, some useful guidelines have been identified to aid the teacher. One important recommendation is to plan and to teach for transfer. A thorough analysis of components of skills which are similar, and an instructional approach which emphasizes these similarities through verbalization, demonstration, or both are useful. Additional guidelines recommend that learners master one skill completely before attempting to begin a new similar one; that similar skills should not be scheduled in close time proximity; and that learners should be helped to understand principles of movement which may be applicable to several skills.

KEY WORDS TO DEFINE OR DESCRIBE

Abilities
Bilateral Transfer
Body Mechanics
Complex Skill
Decision Making
Feedback
Generalization Theory
Identical Elements Theory
Kinematic

Kinetics
Lead-up Activities
Lead-up Games
Mixed Transfer
Motor Plan
Motor Skill
Part Practice
Perception
Physics

Postive Transfer
Principles
Simple Skill
Transfer
Transposition Theory
Whole Practice
Zero Transfer

QUESTIONS FOR DISCUSSION

1. Discuss the use of lead-up games, such as soccer dodge ball or basketball twenty-one, for the promotion of transfer to more complex activities.

2. Discuss the value of experience in a variety of types of movement when the learner attempts to master a specific skill.

3. Why is it important for a teacher to teach for transfer rather than to assume that it will take place automatically?

4. Why is it important for a learner to have mastered a skill before being introduced to a new one which contains some of the same components, but also contains several different components? Referring to the terms postive, negative, and zero transfer, explain your answer to the question.

5. Positive transfer is most likely to occur if the learner can use already learned responses to different stimuli. What type of transfer may take place if new responses must be mastered for stimuli already learned? What type of transfer would be expected if both the stimuli and the responses are different from any previous learning?

6. Consider part to whole and whole to part approaches to instruction. Which of the two approaches would you choose if you were teaching a complex skill? Why?

7. Explain how you would introduce a skill, such as forehand drive in tennis, to learners who have had previous experience in hitting a ball with an implement?

8. Verbalization of the action of a skill appears to facilitate acquisition of that skill by a learner. How might you explain the transfer which appears to occur?

9. Discuss the transfer value of mechanical aids and simulators, such as tennis ball boy machines Account for that value according to the identical elements, generalization, and relationship theories.

10. It is common practice to have learners execute badminton or tennis strokes against a backboard. Is that practice appropriate for positive transfer effects on the actual badminton or tennis court? Explain your answer.

11. Basketball teams, for example, move from court to court during a season of play. One customary practice is for a visiting team to scrimmage on an opponent's home court before an actual game is played. Discuss the value of such a practice. What principles of transfer are involved?

ACTIVITIES

1. A polka step is performed to a 2/4 time signature, counted as 1 and 2. Teach a polka step by demonstrating and verbalizing the rhythmic description of the movement, saying "slide, close, slide" or "left, slide, close" followed by "right, slide, close." The pattern appears as "slide, close, slide." Observe the result. Then teach a different person or group the same pattern by demonstrating and verbalizing only the time pattern of "1 and 2." Comment on the responses obtained. What type of transfer is being employed?

2. Demonstrate a novel skill such as the one described below. Select a learner who has no experience with the skill. Instruct the learner to perform the action with the preferred arm until consistency of the response has been established. At that point direct the learner to execute the same skill with the other arm. Observe the result and comment on the type of transfer which may be involved.

Suggested Novel Skill

Hold a tennis ball in the preferred hand. See Figure 28. Bend the elbow to approximately a 30 degree angle with the hand facing upward toward the ceiling. Let the ball roll from the hand down the forearm until it reaches the elbow space, at that moment straighten the elbow forcefully to cause the ball to bounce about 12" into the air. Catch the ball with the same hand.

3. Using the hierarchal diagrams below and extending those diagrams in Figure 29 as needed, (refer to Section VII, Task Analysis), develop an analysis to show the most critical similarities and differences of, for example, the tennis forehand drive in Diagram A, and those for badminton in Diagram B. Examine the components in the two skills and determine the type of transfer which might be expected from tennis to badminton. (You may substitute skills such as Basketball Tip-in and Volley Ball Dink).

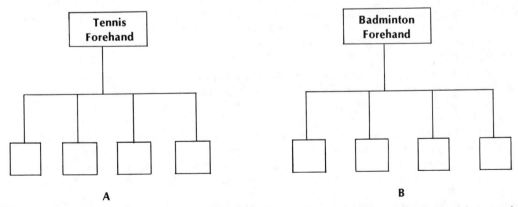

A   B

Note. From **Information Processing in Motor Skills** (p. 174) by R. Marteniuk, 1976, Huntingdon, Cambs: **Lepus Books, Adam and Charles Black (Publishers) Limited. Adapted by permission.**

Figure 29. Hierarchal diagram.

4. Draw a circle with a radius of 2-4 inches in the middle of a blackboard or wall at approximately chest height. Provide a performer with a ball (any size or type). Place the performer at a 45 degree angle to the left of the spot and 6 to 10 feet away from it. Place a second performer, without a ball, in an equivalent position to the right of the spot as in Figure 30. Instruct the performer with the ball to throw the ball toward the spot in such a way that the performer on the right can catch it without moving from the established position. Stop the throwing on the first successful completion of the problem. What principle of transfer might be used to explain the successful result?

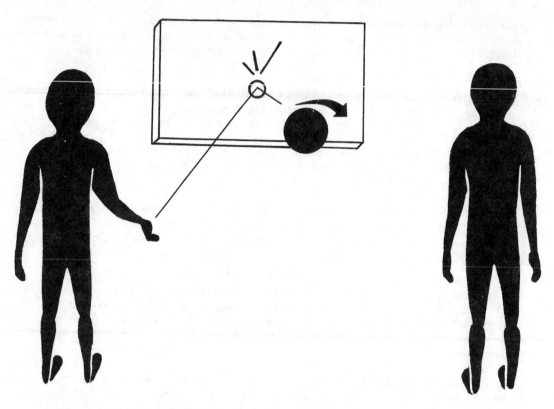

Figure 30. Layout for wall and performers.

5. Select a beginner in tennis who has mastered the grip for the delivery of forehand and backhand strokes, but who is having difficulty with body positioning and timing of the swing for a forehand drive. Using the approach described below, observe the response. Comment on the type of transfer being emphasized.

   Place the markings, as in Figure 31, on the ground or floor and place the learner so that he/she will be inthe relationship to the markings as pictured. Tell the learner to toss the ball upward to make it fall on the "X," while saying "Up," as the ball is tossed up, direct the learner to take a backswing while saying "back;" follow with a step by the foot closest to the net to land on the line drawn while saying "step;" begin the forward swing saying "hit." If the timing is correct, the ball should have bounced and rebounded to its highest point, and the racket will coincidence with it. Continue this practice with the learner repeating rhythmically "Up," "Back," "Step," "Hit" while performing the movements as described.

6. Design a practice drill in a sport skill of your choice (examples are basketball dribble and shoot or field hockey dribble between and around obstacles, traffic cones, persons standing still, etc.) which you judge would be effective for positive transfer. List the principles of transfer which would apply to the drill you have designed.

54

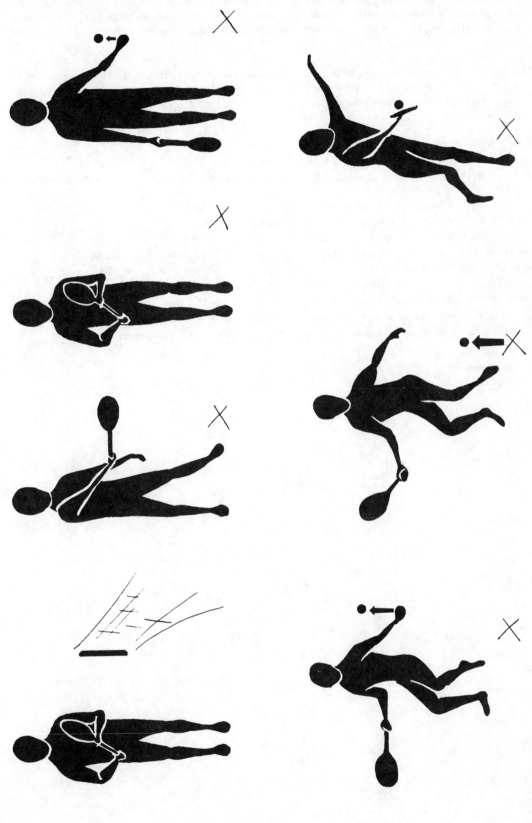

Figure 31. Tennis task.

55

7. Provide a pencil and piece of paper to a learner. Instruct the learner to write his/her name in the usual manner, then try to write the name with the pencil held between the teeth. Use other parts of the body: the toes, the non-preferred hand, etc. Observe the responses. Identify the type of transfer involved.

8. Teach the overhand tennis serve to beginners. Introduce the serve by having the students perform an overhand throw several times with a tennis ball. Then instruct them to use the same motion with the tennis racket in hand. Observe the response. What type of transfer is involved in the approach? Did the expected positive transfer occur?

BIBLIOGRAPHY

Arend, S. (1980). Developing perceptual skills prior to motor performance. *Motor Skills: Theory Into Practice,* 4(1), 11-17.

Arnold-Spaeth, R. K. (1981). Developing sport skills: A dynamic interplay of task, learner, teacher. *Motor Skills: Theory Into Practice* (Monograph 2), pp. 6-7; 69; 79.

Cratty, B. J. (1973). *Teaching motor skills* (pp. 107-116). Englewood Cliffs: Prentice-Hall.

Kerr, R. (1982). *Psychomotor learning* (pp. 67-76). New York: Saunders College Publishing.

Klausmeier, H. J. & Goodwin, W. (1966). *Learning and human abilities* (pp. 462-470). New York: Harper and Row.

Kleinman, M. (1983). *The acquisition of motor skill* (pp. 81-107). Princeton, New Jersey: Princeton Book Company.

Magill, R. A. (1980). *Motor learning: Concepts and applications* (pp. 243-262). Dubuque, IA: William C. Brown.

Marteniuk, R. (1976). *Information processing in motor skills* (pp. 221-223). New York: Holt, Rinehart, and Winston.

Schmidt, R. A. (1982). *Motor control and learning: A behavioral emphasis* (pp. 506-518). Champaign, ILL: Human Kinetics Publishers.

Singer, R. N. (1980). Media and motor learning. *Motor Skills: Theory Into Practice,* 4(2), 95-102.

Stallings, L. (1982). *Motor learning: From theory to practice* (pp. 203-217). St. Louis: The C. V. Mosby Company.

XI. Guide to Understanding Selected Practice Conditions

OVERVIEW AND ORIENTATION

The importance of practice in the acquisition of motor skills is recognized and accepted by both practitioners and researchers. Despite that consensus, scheduling of practice sessions, and methods applied within sessions remain open to question. Teachers, nevertheless, must make decisions about time allotments and instructional approaches which will result in maximum benefit to the learner.

One primary question for a teacher to resolve centers about massing and distributing of practice sessions. Additional questions involve the application of whole and part methods, and the use of mental rehearsal within those sessions. If a massed approach is selected, then there will be provided little or no time between performance trials. The distributed approach would allow actual trials to be short with relatively long rest periods interspersed. If a total skill is practiced, the whole method is being applied. Part practice would involve the performance of components of the whole skill. Where instructions are given to mentally image and covertly rehearse movements, mental practice is being used. It is not unusual to find combinations of time arrangements and method approaches being used in one practice session.

The many operational definitions of terms employed to refer to practice conditions, along with the inclusion of differing levels of learners and tasks in investigations of the topic, have led to a variety of conclusions; however, a few acceptable guidelines have emerged. Within the recommended procedures, the level of the learner and the nature of the skill must be taken into consideration.

Some of the generalizations relating to the level of the learner point up the desirability of using distributed rather than massed practice for beginners and children. For the advanced learner relative massing may be advantageous. Some investigators suggest that beginners, because they are in a cognitive stage of learning, may benefit from mental rehearsal; however, that approach usually is found at advanced stages of learning and performing.

Learners differ in their response to whole and part practice. In general the more advanced the learner, the larger the whole which can be handled successfully. Beginners appear to need part practice. If the skill is such that it cannot be broken down into isolated components without destroying or changing it, then it should be analyzed for the simplest wholes possible for the beginner to absorb.

Guidelines relating to the nature of the skill direct the use of massed practice for skills classified as discrete or relatively simple. Distributed sessions appear to favor the learning of continuous and relatively complex motor tasks. The fatigue which may occur in the execution of such tasks is a factor to be considered when decisions are made to use distributed practice. Sequential or serial type motor tasks in which separation of the parts does not change or destroy the skill may be learned best through part and/or progressive part practices.

There are many combinations of practice conditions which may be planned for relatively complex and simple skills. Fur further discussion of topic, the reader is referred to Cratty (1973, pp. 69-80) and Magill (1980, pp. 278-282). Whatever the schedules and practice conditions selected by the teacher, it should be remembered that they have been demonstrated to affect performance more than learning.

In summary, it is apparent that before selecting the type of practice condition to apply, the teacher

57

should analyze thoroughly both the learner and the motor task to be achieved. While learning may not be a function of the type of practice, performance is. The learner must practice in order to master a motor skill.

KEY WORDS TO DEFINE OR DESCRIBE

Closed Skills

Complex Skill

Continuous Skill

Discrete Skill

Distributed Practice

Learning

Massed Practice

Open Skills

Part Practice

Performance

Progressive Part Practice

Relative Distributing

Relative Massing

Sequential Skills

Simple Skill

Skill Organization

Whole Practice

QUESTIONS FOR DISCUSSION

1. Why is distributed practice appropriate for a beginner?

2. Why may massed practice benefit the advanced learner?

3. What is the difference between performance and learning?

4. What evidence is there that the type of practice appears to affect performance more than learning?

5. Many schools schedule physical education classes to meet two or three times per week, usually with a day between the scheduled days. What type of practice condition does such scheduling represent? Discuss the advantages and disadvantages of such an arrangement for the beginner and for the advanced learner.

6. Given skills such as the overhand tennis serve and the basketball dribble, decide between whole and part practice for each. Support your decision.

7. Given the skills in (6) above placed in the context of a game, decide between massing and distributing the practice. Support your decision.

8. Why is it difficult to determine what are whole and what are part components of motor skills?

9. Discuss the differences in the nature of skills which teachers should recognize when making a decision about teaching by wholes or parts and when determining the probable effectiveness of massed or distributed practices.

10. What are the differences in learners which should be taken into account when decisions about whole and part approaches are made?

11. With what types of skills would the progressive part approach be useful?

12. A typical 40-50 minute physical education class in basketball, for example, may consist of a general warm-up, instruction in one or two specific basketball skills, followed by a scrimmage in which the specific skills are emphasized. The next scheduled class is arranged similarly. Identify the practice conditions being applied.

13. How and when should mental practice be used in the learning of a physical skill? Can a person learn a motor skill through mental practice only? Explain.

ACTIVITIES

1. Analyze the critical components of a basketball lay-up shot from a standing still position, then try to teach that shot to a beginner using the part method: begin with the jump, then shift the ball to position in shooting hand, then push the ball to the backboard to designated point or over the rim of

basket with designated arch to ball. Do *each* part *separately,* then *combine* all parts. Observe the response when all parts are combined. Discuss the result.

2. Repeat exercise (1) above with another beginner but begin with combining all of the parts into a whole so that the movements are continuous with no stops in between. Observe and comment on the effectiveness of the response. Which of the two approaches (1) or (2) appeared to produce the most effective response? Explain.

3. The instructions for the Danish Dance of Greeting executed in 2/4 time are as follows:

Formation: Single circle facing center, hands on hips
Step 1. Clap hands twice, turn to partner and bow
          Clap hands twice, turn to neighbor and bow
Step 2. Stamp right, stamp left; turn in place with four running steps.
Step 3. Repeat Steps 1 and 2.
Step 4. All join hands in large circle and take 16 running steps to the right.
Step 5. Repeat 16 running steps to the left.

Demonstrate the dance as a whole with your own partner, then begin to teach a group of beginners (children) the steps described above, using the progressive part approach. In Figure 32, each segment represents a part, show by numbers of the parts, the progression you would follow. The first two steps are illustrated; complete the plan.

| 1 | | 2 | | 1 + 2 | | 3 | | 1 + 2 + | | 4 | | | | 5 | | |

Note. Bryant J. Cratty, TEACHING MOTOR SKILLS, © **1973, pp. 70-72. Adapted by permission of Prentice-Hall, Inc., Englewood Cliffs, N.J.**

Figure 32. Model for progressive part practice.

4. Many combinations of massed and distributed practice for skill teaching can be developed, one example would be as in Figure 33.

1, 2, 3, 4		5		6		7
Massed Trials		**Distributed Trials**				

Note. Bryant J. Cratty, TEACHING MOTOR SKILLS, © **1973, pp. 70-72. Adapted by permission of Prentice-Hall, Inc., Englewood Cliffs, N.J.**

Figure 33. Model for massed and distributed trials.

Figure 33 shows massing at the beginning, followed by distributed later trials. Develop as many such combinations as you can, then try to assign the best combination to each of the following cases. Offer reasons for the assignment made.

1. Beginners learning to throw darts at target
2. Beginners learning a basketball free throw
3. Beginners learning a headstand
4. Advanced performers practicing a tennis serve
5. Advanced performers practicing forehand and backhand drives on ball sent by opponent

5. Many combinations of whole and part practices may be developed. One example would be as in Figure 34.

Basketball Free Throw	Wrist Action	Basketball Free Throw
Whole Skill	Part of the whole skill	Whole Skill

Note. Bryant J. Cratty, TEACHING MOTOR SKILLS, © 1973, pp. 70-72. Adapted by permission of Prentice-Hall, Inc., Englewood Cliffs, N.J.

Figure 34. Model for whole and part practice.

Figure 34 shows practice of a whole skill which is followed by practice on one of the components of that whole skill, then reintegration of that component into the whole skill for continued practice. Develop as many such combinations as you can, then try to assign the best method to each of the cases cited in (4) above. Offer reasons for your choice.

6. You are a teacher drawing up a plan to teach a three-week block in Volleyball (or any activity of your choice) to a group of Junior High School students who have had no experience with the game. The physical education class hours, each 40-50 minutes long, are scheduled three days a week. Use Figure 35 and show how you would schedule the activity over the three weeks. Include in each block what you would schedule within each class period and the amount of time for each event scheduled within the single class period. Review the completed schedule for appropriateness and effectiveness based on the guidelines for massing and distributing practice and whole and part approaches.

	Monday	Wednesday	Friday
1st Week			
2nd Week			
3rd Week			

Figure 35. Block schedule.

7. Below is a schedule of practice developed by a coach for a high school basketball team:

Number of Minutes	Activity
15	Free shooting and warm-up
10	Grapevine weave
20	Introduce offensive pattern-new skill
30	Practice of offensive pattern just introduced
15	Practice of players by position of the components of offensive pattern applicable to players
10	Shooting drill-lay-up
5	Shooting-foul shots
15	Shooting drill-any combination of shots
(unlimited)	Run mile

Apply guidelines of massed and distributed practice, and part and whole approaches to evaluate the appropriateness of the practice session. What changes, if any, would you make? Explain.

8. Use darts and dartboard (or draw a target on blackboard and provide tennis balls). Direct a learner to *imagine* throwing darts (balls) at the target. The imaging should include when the dart (ball) is first picked up in the hand to the moment it hits the target. Instruct the learner as follows: "Think of how you would throw it. *Follow* its path with your eyes. *Feel* the throw. *See* the dart (ball) *hit the center* of the target. *Think only* of the *dart* (ball), the *path,* the *feeling,* and center of *target."* Direct the learner to take five trials in a two-minute mental practice session. Follow the two-minutes with five actual physical trials. Score the number of hits. Comment on the results. (If you wish to compare results, direct another learner to take five actual physical trials without mental practice, followed by a brief rest, followed by five more actual trials. Score results and compare with first learner.)

BIBLIOGRAPHY

Arnold-Spaeth, R. K. (1981). A dynamic interplay of task, learner, and teacher. *Motor skills: Theory into practice* (Monograph 2), 78-79.

Cratty, B. J. (1973). *Teaching motor skills* (pp. 69-80). Englewood Cliffs: Prentice-Hall.

Klausmeier, H. J. & Goodwin, W. (1966). *Learning and human abilities* (2nd ed.) (pp. 329-339). New York: Harper and Row.

Lawther, J. D. (1977). *The learning and performance of motor skills* (2nd ed.) (pp. 138-153). Englewood cliffs: Prentice-Hall.

Magill, R. A. (1980). *Motor learning: Concepts and applications* (pp. 265-282). Dubuque, IA: William C. Brown.

Rothstein, A., Catelli, L., Dodds, P. & Manahan, J. (1981). *Motor learning: Basic stuff Series I* (pp. 29-43). Washington, DC: American Alliance of Health, Physical Education, Recreation and Dance.

Schmidt, R. A. (1982). *Motor control and learning* (pp. 486-490; 519-521). Champaign, ILL: Human Kinetics Publishers.

Singer, R. N. & Dick, W. (1974). *Teaching physical education: A systems approach* (pp. 193-194). Boston: Houghton Mifflin Company.

Vannier, M. & Gallahue, D. L. (1978). *Teaching physical education in elementary school* (pp. 443-444). Philadelphia: W. B. Saunders Company.

XII. Guide to Understanding the Measurement of Motor Learning

OVERVIEW AND ORIENTATION

Motor learning is defined as "a relatively permanent change in the performance of a motor skill from practice or past experience" (Kerr, 1982, p. 6). Since learning cannot be observed directly, it must be inferred from the overt motor behavior or performance of the learner. As the learner progresses, overt performance should manifest positive behavior changes which persist and are consistent. Evident, also, should be a reduction in muscular tension and effort.

Evaluation of the changes is important for both the student and the teacher. For the student, assessment of progress toward proficiency can be motivational and informative about what is needed to develop further skill. For the teacher, evaluation may serve as an indicator of instructional effectiveness and of changes needed in teaching approaches to facilitate student development.

A variety of measures are employed both singly and in combination to evaluate motor performance. The most commonly used are magnitude of response, speed, accuracy, learning gain, and performance ratings. Examples of response magnitude include the distance or height of a jump, the number of times a forehand is used in a tennis game, or the amount of pressure exerted as in gripping a handle. Speed refers to the amount of time used to complete a given moment or task; for example, the start and completion of a sprint run. Accuracy measures relate to the errors and successes which occur in a motor performance. The number of successful basketball free throws out of a criterion of ten, or the number of feet by which a ball is under or over thrown to a given target are representative of accuracy. Learning gain appraisal is used to evaluate improvement over a span of time. The results of juggling balls for 20 trials of one minute each with one minute rest between trials, or a five-minute dart throwing practice on each of five days would be examples of information to be applied to determine learning gain. Performance ratings and observation protocols usually involve the subjective judgment of observers. The judging of diving and gymnastics events, scatter plots of basketball plays, or form and style effectiveness are representative of subjective assessments. Most often ratings are applied in settings which do not lend themselves to objective measurement. The type of measure or combination of measures selected depend upon the motor task being assessed and the use to be made of the results. The same measures may be employed with individuals and with groups.

The use of the measures defined above yield scores which reflect the type of assessment being employed. Magnitude of response results in a numerical score. A simple count of the number of forehand strokes made in tennis or the number of feet and inches of the jump were cited above as examples. The number of seconds to complete a sprint run becomes a score for the speed example given above. For accuracy tasks, error scores are usually employed. They are numerical measures of distance or time deviations from some standard or criterion. The three error scores used most frequently are absolute error (AE), constant error (CE), and variable error (VE). The first of these AE, is a record of the average amount of error. In the ball example, already cited, the number of feet short and/or long of the target that the five balls land are averaged (See Activity 1 in this section of the Guide). The AE score records only how much error there is. The CE score, sometimes referred to as algebraic error, includes the average of the number of feet that the balls land short of the target, and land long of the target. The computation is an algebraic one because the minus (−) to designate short of the target and the sign plus (+) to designate long of the target are retained (See Activity 2 in this section of the Guide). The retention of the minus (−) and plus (+) signs permit an interpretation of the direction of error. In the example given, CE provides information on whether the balls were underthrown or overthrown. The VE score furnishes insight into the consistency with which an individual or a group performs a motor task. It is a standard deviation score which includes the variation of each ball thrown from the average of the error of all of the five balls thrown (See Activity 3 in this section of the Guide).

Learning scores may be derived in several ways, including the difference in Raw Score, the Total Learning Score, and Percent Gain of Initial Score methods. If the ball juggling example is taken, the number of successful catches during the first of the 20 trials becomes the initial score, with the final score being the number of successful catches in the last of the 20 trials. The learning score would be the successes of the final trial minus (−) the successes of the first trial. The Total Learning Score would be equal to the cumulatively added successes for trials one through 20. The percent of the difference between the sum of the final several trials (e.g., trials 16-20) and the sum of the first several trials (e.g. trials 1-5) would provide the Percent Gain Score (See Activity 8 in this section of the Guide). For a full discussion of learning scores and the preferred methods of computation, the reader is referred to McGraw (1955), Singer (1980), and Lawther (1977).

Scoring of ratings used in the observation of performance depends upon the scale devised or selected. Some require only a check mark to indicate the presence or absence of some feature, others provide numerical values for the quality of movements and/or components of movements. There are many sources which present samples of rating scales. The reader may wish to consult Barrow and McGee (1979).

If a clear representative of performance progress over a period of time is needed, the performance curve, from which a learning trend may be inferred, is helpful. Such a curve is developed by plotting scores made during each practice trial to form a graph. The graph is developed on an ordinate (vertical axis) and an abscissa (horizontal axis) with successes recorded on the ordinate and trials on the abscissa (See Activity 4A in this section of the Guide). Using juggling, again, as an exmaple, a point showing the number of successes in each of the 20 trials would be found on the vertical axis and established over the particular trial shown on the horizontal axis. Once the points have been located, a line is drawn to connect them. The resulting figure is identified as the performance curve. Due to the fact that single trials show great variability from trial to trial, it is useful to average several successive trials to be plotted. That averaging will produce a composite curve which is smoother than the trial to trial configuration. The trend of learning can be seen more easily from the composite curve.

Recently some attention has been given to using an applied behavioral analysis approach to the assessment of motor behavior and change of individual learners. That approach yields a graph or curve which resembles the performance curve; however in behavioral analysis a baseline of the motor behavior being studied must be established through observation or other measures and followed by some intervention (e.g. instruction, equipment, change of motivation, etc.) designed to affect the behavior involved. Behavior following the intervention then is observed or measured and compared with the baseline behavior. Although the resulting graphs can be computed statistically, most often visual analysis of the change in the level and slope of the lines plotted before and after an intervention can provide a rough estimate of progress. Further details of single case designs may be found in Hersen and Barlow (1977) and Zaichowsky (1979).

KEY WORDS TO DEFINE OR DESCRIBE

Abscissa	Error	Motor Learning
Accuracy	Error Scores	Ordinate
Accuracy of Response	Evaluation	Performance
Assessment	Increasing Gains	Performance Curve
Baseline Behavior	Intervention	Physiological Limits
Behavioral Analysis	Learning	Plateau
Composite Curve	Learning Curve	Psychological Limit
Criterion	Level of Line	Rating
Criterion Score	Magnitude of Response	Reaction Time
Decreasing Gains	Measurement	Response Magnitude

Slope of Line   Speed of Response   Visual Analysis
Speed   Target Behavior

QUESTIONS FOR DISCUSSION

1. Why can there be no direct observation of learning?

2. Why may a single performance trial be a poor indication of learning?

3. A high jumper clears the bar at 7 feet. What type of score does the 7 foot achievement represent?

4. Define and differentiate between "learning" and "performance."

5. What would be the general appearance of a success curve for an individual or a group which has progressed in learning?

6. What would you expect the appearance of the curve in #5 above to be if errors were plotted instead of successes.

7. Why is the constant error (CE) score more useful to a teacher than is the absolute error (AE) score?

8. One of the signs that learning of a motor behavior has occurred is the consistency with which a learner performs. Which of the error scores provides information on consistency of performance?

9. What is the difference between reaction time and movement speed?

10. Study the performance curves in Activity 4. Which shape would you expect for a complex skill?

11. If you were measuring the distance between the center of homeplate and the point over which a pitched ball passes over the plate, what type of measure and score would you use?

12. In the case of (11) above, you want to know how long it takes for the ball to travel from the pitcher's hand to homeplate. What type of measure and score would you use?

13. What is the composite performance curve? Why is it a better representation of learning than a trial by trial curve?

14. What is a plateau in a performance curve? In what type of skill is it likely to occur? Why?

15. What is the meaning of physiological limit and psychological limit? At what point are they likely to occur in a performance curve?

16. Consider advantages and disadvantages of the various formulas employed to determine a learning score. What do they suggest to you about evaluation and grading of learners?

17. Why is "performance curve" a more appropriate label than "learning curve?"

18. Explain why a learning curve rarely indicates the extent of learning.

ACTIVITIES

1. This activity provides information and an example of the procedures to be followed in Activities 2 and 3. Recall the ball and target task exemplified in the Overview and Orientation section. Assume that a target is placed 60 ft. (the *standard* or *criterion* distance) from the performer who is to throw five balls at the target for *accuracy*. The performer achieves results as follows:

Trial	Ball Throw	Col. A #ft. from target	Col. B Total #ft. thrown
1	Ball overthrown by 1 foot.	(+1)	61 ft.
2	Ball overthrown by 2 feet.	(+2)	62 ft.
3	Ball overthrown by 2 feet.	(+2)	62 ft.
4	Ball underthrown by 2 feet.	(−2)	58 ft.
5	Ball underthrown by 1 foot.	(−1)	59 ft.

To find the Absolute Error Score (AE), the computation is as follows:

$$AE = \frac{\Sigma[(61\text{-}60) + (62\text{-}60) + (62\text{-}60) + (58\text{-}60) + (59\text{-}60)]}{5}$$

$$AE = \frac{\Sigma[(1) + (2) + (2) + (2) + (1)]}{5}$$

$$AE = \frac{8}{5} = 1.6 \text{ ft.}$$

The thrower missed the target on the average of 1.6 ft. over the 5 trials. The plus (+) and minus (−) score designations are disregarded. The formula for AE is:

$$AE = \frac{\Sigma\left[\left(\begin{matrix}\text{Distance - Criterion}\\ \text{thrown,}\quad\text{Distance}\\ \text{Trial 1}\end{matrix}\right) + \ldots \left(\begin{matrix}\text{Distance - Criterion}\\ \text{thrown,}\quad\text{Distance}\\ \text{Trial 5}\end{matrix}\right)\right]}{\text{Number of Trials}} \quad (1)$$

Complete formula (1) using the space below, to include trials 2, 3, and 4.

2. Using the scores earned on trials and Column A in (1) above, *complete* the formula (2) and *complete* the result. Be sure to *retain* plus (+) and minus (−) signs. Interpret the score. Does the score provide a more accurate picture of performers than the score in (1) above? Explain.

$$CE = \frac{\Sigma\left[\left(\begin{matrix}\text{Distance - Criterion}\\ \text{thrown,}\quad\text{Distance}\\ \text{Trial 1}\end{matrix}\right) + \ldots \left(\begin{matrix}\text{Distance - Criterion}\\ \text{thrown,}\quad\text{Distance}\\ \text{Trial 5}\end{matrix}\right)\right]}{\text{Number of Trials}} \quad (2)$$

3. Using the scores earned on trials and Column A in (1) above with the CE result in (2) above, *complete* formula (3) and *compute* the result. Interpret the score. What information does the score provide? How would it help the teacher to determine progress being made in learning?

$$VE = \sqrt{\frac{\Sigma\left[\left(\begin{matrix}\text{Signed score,}\\ \text{Trial 1}\end{matrix} - CE\right)^2 + \ldots \left(\begin{matrix}\text{Signed score,}\\ \text{Trial 5}\end{matrix} - CE\right)^2\right]}{\text{Number of Trials}}} \quad (3)$$

65

4. Study the prototypes of performance curves as shown in Figure 36, then answer 4A, B, C, D, E.

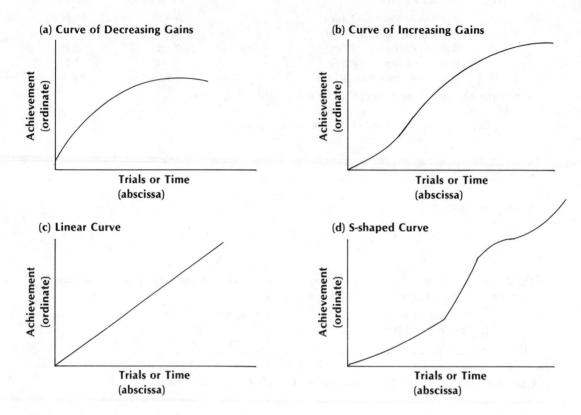

(a) Curve of Decreasing Gains

Achievement (ordinate)

Trials or Time (abscissa)

(b) Curve of Increasing Gains

Achievement (ordinate)

Trials or Time (abscissa)

(c) Linear Curve

Achievement (ordinate)

Trials or Time (abscissa)

(d) S-shaped Curve

Achievement (ordinate)

Trials or Time (abscissa)

Figure 36. Prototypes of curves.

A. Consider that 20 one-minute trials have been performed in a juggling task with the following results:

Trial	Successes	Errors	Trial	Successes	Errors
1	5	10	11	10	5
2	6	11	12	16	3
3	6	9	13	18	3
4	3	8	14	12	4
5	8	8	15	21	3
6	11	7	16	21	2
7	5	7	17	24	2
8	12	6	18	24	1
9	12	7	19	24	1
10	12	5	20	24	1

Plot a curve showing the number of successes on the graph provided in Figure 37.

B. Identify the type of curve obtained (refer to prototypes in Figure 36).

C. From the curve, can you determine the relative complexity of the skill and/or the level of the learner? Explain.

D. Is there a plateau in the curve? If so, Why?

E. Does the curve show that a "physiological" and/or "psychological" limit has been reached?

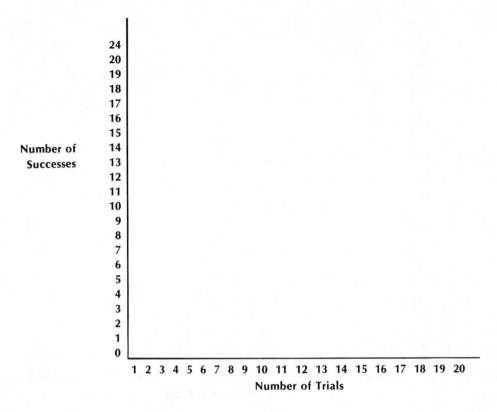

Figure 37. Graph to plot curve.

5. Use the error scores listed in (4A) above and plot a curve, using a dotted (----) line, on the graph developed on Figure 37. Compare, by visual inspection, the success and error curves. What can you state about learning?

6. Group the success scores listed in (4A) above into blocks of four and average each block. Plot the results in Figure 38.

    Compare the curve obtained to that of (4A) above. Which of the two curves provide a better representation of improvement? Why?

7. The difference learning score for the juggling task of (4A) above would be 19. Cumulatively add scores for trials 1-20 and obtain the true learning score.

8. Compute learning scores for percent gain, formula (4), using the average of the first three trials and the average of the final three trials and criterion of 30 in the formula.

$$\frac{\text{(sum of last "n . . ." trials) - (sum of first "n . . ." trials)}}{\text{(Highest possible score on "n . . ." trials) - (sum of first "n . . ." trials)}} \qquad (4)$$

    Compare results of (7) above with this result. Which one provides the better information to the teacher? Why?

9. Observe a beginner executing sets of five basketball free throws for five sets. Record the success or error of five balls on Figure 39 beginning with the *first* ball of every *set of five*. Try to observe errors in performance which inhibit complete success. After 10 minutes, provide corrective instructions, permit several trials, then observe again for 10 minutes. Plot the results on the diagram in Figure 39, Discuss changes observed in the *slope* and *level* of the line plotted after instructions are given.

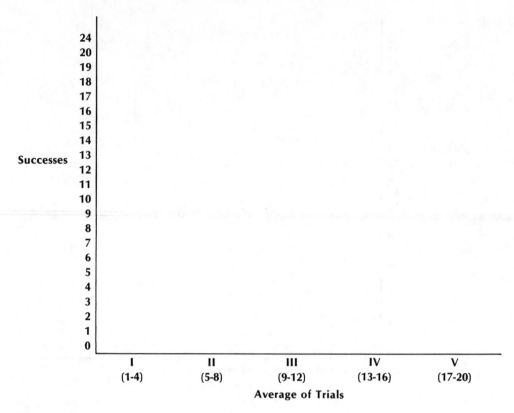

Figure 38. Composite graph.

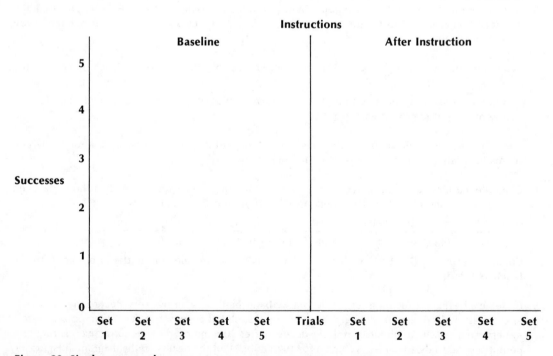

Figure 39. Single case graph.

BIBLIOGRAPHY

Barrow, H. M. & McGee, R. (1979). *A practical approach to measurement in physical education* (3rd ed.) (pp. 252-165). Philadelphia: Lea & Febiger.

Cratty, B. J. (1973). *The teaching of motor skills* (pp. 39-41). Englewood Cliffs: Prentice-Hall.

Dodds, P. (1978). Behavior analysis of students: What students can tell teachers without ever saying a word. *Motor Skills: Theory into Practice, 3*(1), 3-10.

Garry, R. & Kingsley, H. L. (1970). *The nature and conditions of learning* (pp. 60-66). Englewood Cliffs: Prentice-Hall.

Hersen, M. & Barlow, D. H. (1977). *Single case experimental designs* (pp. 47-50); 278-282). New York: Pergamon Press.

Kerr, R. (1982). *Psychomotor learning* (pp. 5-6). New York: Saunders College Publishing.

Kerr, R. & Smoll, F. L. (1977). Variability in individual student performance: Implications for teachers. *Motor Skills: Theory into Practice, 1*(2), 75-86.

Klausmeier, H. J. & Goodwin, W. (1961). *Learning and human abilities* (pp. 621-639). Harper and Row.

Knapp, B. (1970). *Skill in sport* (pp. 7-15). London: Routledge and Kegan Paul.

Komaki, J. L. (1982). Single case experimental designs: Evaluations without traditional control groups. *Psychology of Motor Behavior and Sport.* College Park, MD: University of Maryland.

McGraw, L. W. (1955). Comparative analysis of methods of scoring tests of motor learning. *Research Quarterly, 26,* 440-453.

Rothstein, A., Catelli, L. Dodds, P. & Manahan, J. (1981). *Motor learning: Basic stuff Series I* (pp. 55-62). Reston, VA: AAHPERD.

Rife, F. & Dodd, S. P. (1978). Developing evidential bases for educational practice through single subject research paradigm. *Motor Skills: Theory into Practice, 3*(1), 40-48.

Schmidt, R. A. (1982). *Motor control and learning* (pp. 438-439). Champaign, IL: Human Kinetics Publishers.

Singer, R. N. (1982). *The learning of motor skills* (pp. 35-37); 42-45). New York: MacMillan Publishing Company.

Zaichowsky, L. D. (1980). Single case experimental designs and sport psychology. In C. H. Nadeau, W. R. Halliwell, K. M. Newell, & G. C. Roberts (Eds.) *Psychology of Motor Behavior and Sport.* Champaign, ILL: Human Kinetics Publishers.